SMP 16–19

Statistics 2

Distributions and hypothesis testing

CAMBRIDGE
UNIVERSITY PRESS

This book is adapted from earlier SMP books, with additional material, by Sue Glover.
Other material was originally contributed by

Chris Belsom
Robert Black
David Cundy
Stan Dolan
Judith Galsworthy
Andy Hall
Mike Hall
Ron Haydock
Janet Jagger
Ann Kitchen
Chris Little
Fiona McGill

Melissa Rodd
Paul Roder
Tom Roper
Mary Rouncefield
Mike Savage
Jane Southern
Bernard Taylor
Carole Tyler
Nigel Walkey
Nigel Webb
Julian Williams
Phil Wood

PUBLISHED BY THE PRESS SYNDICATE OF THE UNIVERSITY OF CAMBRIDGE
The Pitt Building, Trumpington Street, Cambridge, United Kingdom

CAMBRIDGE UNIVERSITY PRESS
The Edinburgh Building, Cambridge, CB2 2RU, UK
40 West 20th Street, New York, NY 10011–4211, USA
477 Williamstown Road, Port Melbourne, VIC 3207, Australia
Ruiz de Alarcón 13, 28014 Madrid, Spain
Dock House, The Waterfront, Cape Town 8001, South Africa

http://www.cambridge.org

First published 2002

Printed in the United Kingdom at the University Press, Cambridge

Typeface Minion and Officina   *System* QuarkXpress®

A catalogue record for this book is available from the British Library

ISBN 0 521 78803 X paperback

Cover photograph: Peter Menzel/Science Photo Library
Cover design: Angela Ashton

Contents

Using this book

Most sections within a chapter consist of work developing new ideas followed by an exercise for practice in using those ideas.

Within the development sections, some questions and activities are labelled with a **D**, for example **2D**, and are enclosed in a box. These involve issues that are worth exploring through discussion – either teacher-led discussion in the whole class or discussion by students in small groups, who may then feed back their conclusions to the whole class.

Questions labelled **E** are more demanding.

Statistical tables are included in this book, but students should familiarise themselves with the tables which will be provided for the examination. Layouts, numbers of significant figures and definitions can all vary.

1 Goodness of fit: the chi-squared test

A How good is a probabilistic model? (answers p. 81)

Some mathematical models are **deterministic** in nature. They provide exact information which can be used to predict future behaviour. For example, the path of a cricket ball can be modelled by equations of motion based on the laws of Newtonian mechanics. Various assumptions will be made. For example, you can treat the ball as a particle and so ignore spin; you can ignore frictional forces, or perhaps model them in some way (for example, as being proportional to the speed of the ball); and so on. Once the assumptions are made clear, however, the equation of motion which is produced by the mathematical model can be used to predict such things as time of flight, maximum height and range.

The Newtonian model of the solar system is regarded as a good model because predictions of events such as eclipses can be made with extreme accuracy. The 'goodness of fit' of any model can be assessed by considering how well the predictions fit in with actual events.

Statistical data are not deterministic in nature, but are subject to random variation so that you cannot predict future values with certainty. However, long-term relative frequencies of events closely match predictable patterns, i.e. there is 'order from chaos'.

For example, although the path a ball takes through a binostat is unpredictable, when the experiment is repeated with a large number of balls, the relative frequencies of the balls exhibit a pattern which can be modelled mathematically.

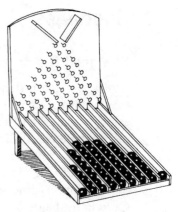

Although the values of statistical data can never be predicted with certainty, you can model relative frequencies with probabilities. You can then use the resulting **probability models** to make predictions and inferences. These will not have the exactness of a deterministic model, but their degree of uncertainty can be measured.

1D Which of the following situations are more likely to be successfully modelled with a deterministic mathematical model and which with a probabilistic mathematical model?

(a) The number of matches in a matchbox

(b) The amount the pound in your pocket will be worth in five years' time

(c) The flight of a space probe to the planet Mars

(d) The result of the next general election

(e) The rate of a nuclear reaction

(f) Whether a new baby is a boy or girl

It is relatively easy to evaluate the appropriateness of a deterministic model: you can see if its predictions turn out to be true! With a probabilistic model, this is not so easy since it deals with uncertainties.

Example 1

Two dice are thrown and the positive difference between their scores recorded. Calculate the expected frequencies for the difference in 600 such throws.

Solution

The table lists all the possible number pairs and the difference each produces.

		First dice					
		1	2	3	4	5	6
	1	0	1	2	3	4	5
	2	1	0	1	2	3	4
Second	3	2	1	0	1	2	3
dice	4	3	2	1	0	1	2
	5	4	3	2	1	0	1
	6	5	4	3	2	1	0

From this table, you can count the number of ways differences can occur and hence obtain the associated probabilities as shown in the next table.

Difference	0	1	2	3	4	5
Number of ways	6	10	8	6	4	2
Probability	$\frac{3}{18}$	$\frac{5}{18}$	$\frac{4}{18}$	$\frac{3}{18}$	$\frac{2}{18}$	$\frac{1}{18}$
Expected frequency	100	167	133	100	67	33

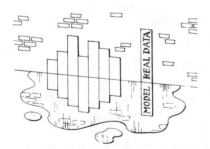

$\frac{3}{18} \times 600 =$ expected frequency
$= 100$

How good is the model?

Suppose you have proposed a probability model and deduced expected frequencies. You could compare these with observed data. But how close should you *expect* these to be? How 'good' is the fit?

A measure of 'goodness of fit' which will give some idea of how far the observed frequencies are from the expected frequencies, and whether the discrepancy is 'reasonable', is introduced below.

If you wanted to check whether a dice was biased towards scoring a six or a one, you could throw it, for example 1200 times, and record the number of ones, sixes and other scores.

Suppose you obtained the results below for dice A, B, C and D (which was thrown only 600 times).

Dice A	1	6	Other		Dice B	1	6	Other
Observed	182	238	780		Observed	201	199	800
Expected	200	200	800		Expected	200	200	800

Dice C	1	6	Other		Dice D	1	6	Other
Observed	220	218	762		Observed	120	118	362
Expected	200	200	800		Expected	100	100	400

2   Explain why the expected frequencies for an unbiased dice would be 200 ones, 200 sixes and 800 other scores for 1200 throws.

3   Which of the dice A, B, C and D appear to be biased?

A measure of 'goodness of fit' is needed which confirms an intuitive idea of how biased the dice appear to be.

4   One possibility would be to calculate the deviation (+ or −) between observed and expected frequency for each category, or cell, and then sum these.

(a) Calculate this for dice A.

(b) Why is it not a satisfactory measure?

5   To improve the measure used in question 3, you could square the deviations, then add. You could write this measure as

$$\Sigma \, (\text{observed} - \text{expected})^2$$

where the sum is across all the categories or cells.

(a) Calculate $\Sigma \, (\text{observed} - \text{expected})^2$ for each dice.

(b) Compare the results for dice C and dice D. Why is this measure not satisfactory?

(c) Compare the results for dice A and dice C. Why is this measure not satisfactory?

A better measure is obtained by dividing the squared differences in each cell *by the expected frequency for that cell*. This gives the statistic

$$\Sigma \, \frac{(\text{observed} - \text{expected})^2}{\text{expected}}$$

For dice A, this works out as

$$\frac{(182 - 200)^2}{200} + \frac{(238 - 200)^2}{200} + \frac{(780 - 800)^2}{800} = 9.34$$

This **goodness of fit** statistic is usually denoted by X^2. (The reason for this choice of symbol will become apparent later.)

6 (a) Calculate X^2 for the dice B, C and D.

(b) List all four dice in order of increasing value of X^2.

The larger the value of X^2 obtained, the further the observed frequencies deviate from the expected frequencies for an unbiased dice, and hence the more likely it is that the dice is biased.

The X^2 results for the dice A, B, C and D should confirm your intuition about which are more likely to be biased.

A measure of goodness of fit is obtained by dividing the square of the difference between each observed and expected frequency by the expected frequency and then adding together the results.

The 'goodness of fit' test statistic, X^2, is defined by

$$X^2 = \sum_i \frac{(O_i - E_i)^2}{E_i}$$

O stands for 'Observed frequency'

E stands for 'Expected frequency'

Exercise A (answers p. 81)

1 (a) Calculate X^2 for the birth data in the table for each of these assumptions.

    (i) $P(\text{boy}) = P(\text{girl}) = 0.5$

    (ii) $P(\text{boy}) = 0.513$

	Boy first	Girl first
Boy second	31	21
Girl second	22	26

(b) Which model in (a) gives the closer fit?

2 Before you can start a game of 'snakes and ladders', you need to throw a six. The following data are for the number of throws taken to get the six you need to start the game.

Number of throws to get a six	1	2	3	4	5	6 or more	
Frequency	25	24	23	22	15	91	Total = 200

Let N be the number of throws until a six is obtained.

(a) Using a tree diagram or otherwise, show the following are true.
   (i) $P(N=1) = \frac{1}{6}$
   (ii) $P(N=2) = (\frac{5}{6})(\frac{1}{6})$
   (iii) $P(N=3) = (\frac{5}{6})^2(\frac{1}{6})$

(b) Deduce the probability distribution for N and calculate the expected frequencies corresponding to the observed frequencies.

(c) Calculate X^2 for the given data.

3   At the local library, the number of books loaned on each day of a particular week are given in the table.

Monday	Tuesday	Wednesday	Thursday	Friday	Saturday
200	290	250	285	265	270

Calculate X^2 on the basis of a probability model which assumes that books are equally likely to be borrowed on any day.

4   Three coins were tossed 800 times and the number of heads recorded. The following data were obtained.

Number of heads	0	1	2	3
Frequency	78	255	341	126

(a) Construct a probability model for this situation and calculate the expected frequencies.

(b) Calculate X^2 for the data.

B The chi-squared distribution (answers p. 82)

You have now met a statistic, X^2, for measuring the 'goodness of fit' of a probability model when applied to data.

$$X^2 = \sum_i \frac{(O_i - E_i)^2}{E_i}$$ O stands for observed frequency

E stands for expected frequency

Thus for dice A (in Section A above), assuming it is unbiased, you calculated X^2 as 9.34 for the following data.

Dice A	1	6	Other
Observed	182	238	780
Expected	200	200	800

Similarly, for dice B, C and D, the X^2 values were 0.01, 5.42 and 10.85 respectively. These values suggest that dice D is the most likely to be biased.

The data for dice A shown above refer to a single data collection of 1200 throws, and the value of $X^2 = 9.34$ is specific to this data collection. If the same dice was thrown 1200 times again then you would almost certainly obtain a different set of results and therefore a different value of X^2 for dice A. Clearly, X^2 will be different for every data collection – it will have its own distribution of values. The greater X^2 is, the worse is the fit of the model to the data. The question you need to answer is: how high does X^2 have to be before you should become unhappy with the fit of the probability model to the data?

To answer this question you need to consider the *distribution* of X^2 which, fortunately, can be modelled mathematically. It can be approximated by one of a family of distributions known as the **chi-squared (χ^2) distributions**, written $\chi^2(1)$, $\chi^2(2)$, $\chi^2(3)$ and so on. (χ (chi) is the Greek letter x: hence the use of X^2 in the 'goodness of fit' statistic.)

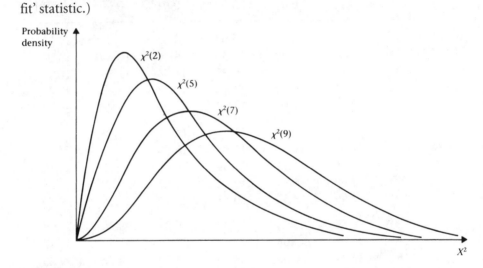

The n of $\chi^2(n)$ is known as the number of **degrees of freedom** and is often denoted by the Greek letter ν (nu). It is calculated as follows for dice D.

Score	1	6	Other
Frequency	120	118	362

Once the frequencies for score 1 and score 6 are known, the frequency of the other scores is fixed as $600 - (120 + 118)$, so the relevant χ^2 distribution has two degrees of freedom ($\nu = 2$).

The actual mathematical function for $\chi^2(\nu)$ is complicated. In practice, as in the case of the Normal distribution (*Statistics 1*, Chapter 3), all you need to know is how the area is distributed.

A typical table of χ^2 probabilities is illustrated on the next page.

The tabulated value is χ_p^2, where $P(X^2 > \chi_p^2) = p$, when X^2 has a χ^2 distribution with ν degrees of freedom

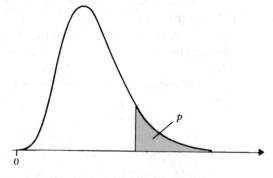

The tables provided for use in the examination may also give lower percentage points, and may define p as $P(X^2 < \chi_p^2) = p$.

p	0.1	0.05	0.025	0.01	0.005	0.001
$\nu = 1$	2.71	3.84	5.02	6.63	7.88	10.83
2	4.61	5.99	7.38	9.21	10.60	13.81
3	6.25	7.81	9.35	11.34	12.84	16.27
4	7.78	9.49	11.14	13.28	14.86	18.47
5	9.24	11.07	12.83	15.09	16.75	20.52
6	10.64	12.59	14.45	16.81	18.55	22.46
7	12.02	14.07	16.01	18.48	20.28	24.32
8	13.36	15.51	17.53	20.09	21.95	26.12
9	14.68	16.92	19.02	21.67	23.59	27.88
10	15.99	18.31	20.48	23.21	25.19	29.59
12	18.55	21.03	23.34	26.22	28.30	32.91
14	21.06	23.68	26.12	29.14	31.32	36.12
16	23.54	26.30	28.85	32.00	34.27	39.25
18	25.99	28.87	31.53	34.81	37.16	42.31
20	28.41	31.41	34.17	37.57	40.00	45.31
25	34.38	37.65	40.65	44.31	46.93	52.62
30	40.26	43.77	46.98	50.89	53.67	59.70
40	51.81	55.76	59.34	63.69	66.77	73.40
50	63.17	67.50	71.42	76.15	79.49	86.66
60	74.40	79.08	83.30	88.38	91.95	99.61
100	118.5	124.3	129.6	135.8	140.2	149.4

The table shows, for any χ^2 function, the proportion of the area which lies to the right of certain values of X^2.

Graph of the χ^2 density function for $\nu = 12$

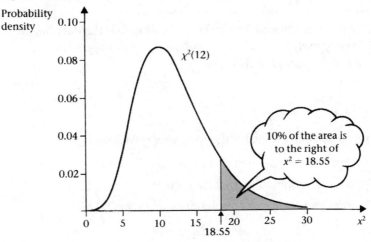

This means that the probability of obtaining a value of $\chi^2(12)$ greater than 18.55 is 0.1.

1   Find the value 18.55 in the table on page 8. Find also the following values.

(a) The value of $\chi^2(12)$ which has 1% of the area to the right

(b) The value of $\chi^2(5)$ which has 5% of the area to the right

You are now in a position to make some judgement on each of the dice considered in Section A. For dice A the observed data led to an X^2 value of 9.34. There are only two degrees of freedom, so consider $\chi^2(2)$.

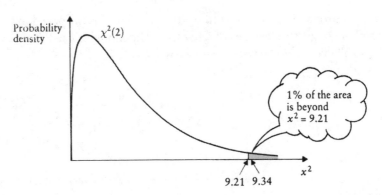

A value of X^2 greater than 9.21 would occur in fewer than 1% of cases. This suggests that the model used for dice A (that of an unbiased dice) is *not* a good fit to the real data. The difference between the expected and observed frequencies is high, and such a high value for X^2 would

occur in fewer than 1% of cases by chance alone. There is strong evidence to suggest that dice A is biased.

2 Consider the other dice in the same way.

3D For dice B, we calculated $X^2 = 0.01$, indicating that the data fits the model very closely. Would such results cause you to question the accuracy of the model in this case?

Exercise B (answers p. 83)

Use a χ^2 probability table for the following questions.

1 X^2 has a χ^2 distribution with five degrees of freedom.

(a) What is the probability that X^2 is greater than 12.83?

(b) In what percentage of samples does X^2 exceed 11.07?

2 X^2 has a χ^2 distribution with ten degrees of freedom.

(a) X^2 exceeds the value a in 5% of samples. Find a.

(b) There is a 2.5% probability of X^2 exceeding the value c. Find c.

C Testing a model: the chi-squared test (answers p. 83)

In a project to investigate the distribution of the number of girls in families, the following data were obtained for families having three children.

Number of girls	0	1	2	3	
Number of families	9	17	21	4	Total = 51 families

A binomial probability model, with $p = 0.5$ and $n = 3$, is proposed for the numbers of girls in families of size three. The model is used as a basis for calculating the *expected frequencies*.

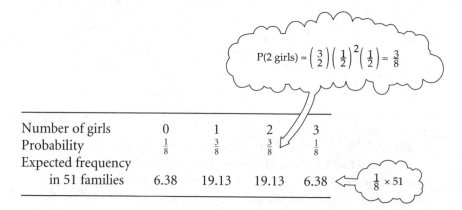

$$P(2 \text{ girls}) = \left(\begin{array}{c}3\\2\end{array}\right)\left(\frac{1}{2}\right)^2\left(\frac{1}{2}\right) = \frac{3}{8}$$

Number of girls	0	1	2	3
Probability	$\frac{1}{8}$	$\frac{3}{8}$	$\frac{3}{8}$	$\frac{1}{8}$
Expected frequency in 51 families	6.38	19.13	19.13	6.38

$\frac{1}{8} \times 51$

$$X^2 = \sum \frac{(O - E)^2}{E}$$

$$= \frac{(9 - 6.38)^2}{6.38} + \frac{(17 - 19.13)^2}{19.13} + \frac{(21 - 19.13)^2}{19.13} + \frac{(4 - 6.38)^2}{6.38}$$

$$= 2.38$$

There are four cells in the table. In this case, the number of degrees of freedom is $4 - 1 = 3$. From tables of $\chi^2(3)$, the 5% (or 0.05) value of X^2 is 7.81 . The value obtained (2.38) is well below this value and so is not unusual. This suggests good agreement between the model and the real data. The result is said to be **not significant**.

If you obtain a value for X^2 greater than 7.81, then the difference between the values predicted by the model and those actually observed (the real data) would have been greater than would have been expected by chance variation alone. The model seems inappropriate for the data. In such a case, the result is described as **significant at the 5% level**.

A word of warning here – the χ^2 test as described above should only be used if the expected frequency of a cell is 5 or more. Otherwise, groups/cells must be combined. The total frequency should also be 50 or more.

The χ^2 test should only be used if

- the expected frequency of each cell is *5 or more*
- the total frequency is *50 or more.*

Deciding on the correct number of degrees of freedom is crucial in choosing the appropriate χ^2 distribution with which to test the model.

The number of degrees of freedom is the number of *independent* cells used to calculate the value of X^2 . This is equal to the number of cells minus the number of constraints. For example, in a dice experiment where you record ones, sixes and other scores in 120 throws, you might obtain

Score	1	6	Others	
Frequency	25	18	77	Total = 120

Here, there are three cells and one constraint (that the total is 120). Therefore there are $3 - 1 = 2$ degrees of freedom.

Further constraints on the observed frequencies are considered below.

The following data for the distribution of girls in 51 families of three children were considered earlier.

Number of girls	0	1	2	3
Number of families	9	17	21	4

If you assume that boys and girls are equally likely to be born ($p = 0.5$), then the binomial model gives a value of $X^2 = 2.38$.

Instead, you could *use the data* to estimate the proportion of girls and then model the data with a binomial distribution using this estimate for p.

1 (a) Show that the total number of girls in this sample is 71.

   (b) Show that the proportion of girls in the sample is 0.464.

   (c) Using this value as an estimate of p, the proportion of girls in the population, complete the binomial probability distribution and the expected frequencies in the following table.

Number of girls per family	0	1	2	3
Probability	0.154	0.400		
Expected frequency	7.85	20.4		

2 (a) Calculate the value of X^2 for the model above.

   (b) Confirm that this is lower than the value obtained by taking $p = 0.5$.
   Why do you think this is?

There is now an extra constraint on the observed frequencies. Not only does the total observed frequency have to be 51; in addition, the total number of girls must be 71, to give the estimated probability of 0.464.

3 Given these two constraints and the first two observed frequencies of 9 and 17, deduce that the other two observed frequencies *must* be 21 and 4 respectively.

By estimating the proportion p from the observed frequencies, an extra constraint has been added to the observed frequencies – you are now using the constraints '71 girls among 51 families' as opposed to just '51 families'. The number of degrees of freedom is therefore reduced by one. There are four cells and two constraints, giving $4 - 2 = 2$ degrees of freedom. The correct distribution for X^2 in this case is $\chi^2(2)$.

Either model for the number of girls per family still fits the observed data. ($2.38 < 7.81$ and $1.61 < 5.99$, so the results are not significant at the 5% level.)

$$\text{Number of degrees of freedom} = \text{number of cells} - \text{number of constraints}$$

Since the total frequency is fixed, this is always a constraint. In addition, each time the data are used to estimate a parameter for the model (such as p in the binomial model), this adds another constraint and reduces the number of degrees of freedom by one. For example, suppose you had collected the following data on the number of girls in 100 families of size four.

Number of girls	0	1	2	3	4	
Number of families	5	24	37	30	4	Total = 100

If you were to compare these data with the frequencies expected on the basis of using $B(4, \frac{1}{2})$ for the number of girls in each family, then the number of degrees of freedom is:

$$\nu = \text{number of cells} - 1 = 4$$

If, instead, you were to use $B(4, p)$ with p calculated from the data as $\frac{204}{400} = 0.51$, then there would be the extra constraint that the mean of the model must equal the mean of the data, and

$$\nu = 5 - 2 = 3$$

Exercise C (answers p. 83)

1   According to Mendel's theory of genetics, the number of peas of a certain variety which fall into the classifications round and yellow, wrinkled and yellow, round and green, and wrinkled and green should be in the ratio $9 : 3 : 3 : 1$. Suppose that for 100 such peas, 55, 20, 16 and 9 were in these respective classes. Do these results agree with Mendelian theory?

2   Imported peaches come in boxes each holding six peaches. A batch of 100 boxes in a supermarket revealed the following distribution of imperfect fruit amongst the boxes.

No. of imperfect peaches in box	0	1	2	3	4	5	6
Frequency	49	24	14	9	3	1	0

Use the data to estimate the proportion of imperfect peaches. Use this to calculate the expected frequency of boxes out of 100 with 0, 1, 2 and 3 or more imperfect peaches (assume statistical independence). Then conduct a χ^2 goodness of fit test on these four cells, and test the model.

3   Four coins are tossed 100 times and the number of heads (H) counted each time. The results are as follows.

No. of heads (H)	0	1	2	3	4
Frequency	5	21	32	34	8

(a) Test the data against the model $H \sim B(4, \frac{1}{2})$.

(b) Estimate p (the probability of obtaining a head when a coin is thrown) from the data. Test the data against the model $H \sim B(4, p)$.

Comment on your results in (a) and (b).

D   Contingency tables (answers p. 84)

In much of this book you will be looking at a range of probability models which can be used to model data. The χ^2 goodness of fit test can be used as a check to see if a model is appropriate, or to see if the assumptions behind a model are reasonable.

This section considers a common and useful application of χ^2 which tests the *independence* of two characteristics.

Here are some data on voting intentions for a council election in a small rural community. They are classified according to the age of the voters. There were only two candidates, one Labour and one Conservative. 'Don't knows' were discounted.

		Age (years)			
	18–25	26–40	41–60	60+	Total
Will vote Labour	5	27	13	21	66
Will vote Conservative	14	35	47	56	152
Total	19	62	60	77	218

This sort of two-way table is called a **contingency table**.

A total of 66 out of 218 intend to vote Labour and 152 out of 218 intend to vote Conservative. *Assuming that age does not affect voting intention*, you would expect the following frequencies in the 18–25 category.

Will vote Labour	$19 \times \frac{66}{218} = 5.8$
Will vote Conservative	$19 \times \frac{152}{218} = 13.2$
	Total $= 19$

1 Calculate expected frequencies for the remaining age categories and hence complete the following table of expected frequencies.

	18–25	26–40	41–60	60+	Total
Will vote Labour	5.8				66
Will vote Conservative	13.2				152
Total	19	62	60	77	218

2 Calculate $X^2 = \sum \dfrac{(O-E)^2}{E}$ for the eight cells of the table.

In determining the expected frequencies, both the row totals (to determine the overall proportion of Labour/Conservative voters) and the column totals (to calculate the expected frequencies in each age category) have been used. So these are fixed constraints on the observed frequencies in this table.

	18–25	26–40	41–60	60+	Total
Will vote Labour					66
Will vote Conservative					152
Total	19	62	60	77	218

In this case, once three observed frequencies are known, the others are determined by the row and column totals. Therefore, $v = 3$.

3 Complete the χ^2 test and comment on whether voting intention is related to age.

You can generalise to find a rule for the number of degrees of freedom in this sort of test. The row and column totals are fixed in determining the model. Suppose you had a four by five table, as follows.

Observed table of values

	A	B	C	D	E	Total
i						fixed
ii						fixed
iii						fixed
iv						fixed
Total	fixed	fixed	fixed	fixed	fixed	

There are only three **free entries** in each column; the fourth entry is fixed so that the total for the column agrees with the observed data.

Similarly each row has only four free entries, as the row total must agree with the observed data. In this 4 × 5 contingency table there will be 3 × 4 = 12 free entries, so that the table has 12 degrees of freedom. This result may be generalised:

> In an $m \times n$ contingency table there will be $(m-1)(n-1)$ degrees of freedom.

The χ^2 distribution is used to test the calculated value of X^2 for the data. Conditions on its use are that the *expected frequency* of each cell must be 5 or more and that the *total frequency* should be at least 50. Under such conditions, χ^2 satisfactorily models the distribution of the difference measure, X^2. However, the approximation is less good when there is only one degree of freedom. This is always the case for 2 × 2 contingency tables. A correction to improve the fit, known as **Yates' correction**, can then be used.

> If the number of degrees of freedom ν is 1, then using **Yates' correction**
>
> $$X^2 = \sum_i \frac{(|O_i - E_i| - 0.5)^2}{E_i}$$

Example 2

In a trial, 120 out of 200 women can distinguish margarine from butter, whereas 108 out of 200 men can tell the difference. Does this trial provide evidence of a gender-related difference in taste discrimination?

Solution

The data can be expressed in a 2 × 2 contingency table.

	Men	Women	Total
Can tell	108	120	228
Cannot tell	92	80	172
Total	200	200	400

A model based on the assumption that there is no difference in the ability of men and women to distinguish between butter and margarine would lead to the following expected frequencies:

	Men	Women	
Can tell	114	114	228
Cannot tell	86	86	172
Total	200	200	400

$\frac{228}{400}$ can tell the difference. You would expect $\frac{228}{400}$ of the 200 women to be able to do so i.e. $\frac{228}{400} \times 200 = 114$

Calculating the difference measure and using Yates' correction:

$$X^2 = \sum_i \frac{(|O_i - E_i| - 0.5)^2}{E_i}$$

$$= \frac{(|108 - 114| - 0.5)^2}{114} + \frac{(|120 - 114| - 0.5)^2}{114}$$

$$+ \frac{(|92 - 86| - 0.5)^2}{86} + \frac{(|80 - 86| - 0.5)^2}{86}$$

= 1.23 with one degree of freedom

As this value does not exceed the $\chi^2(1)$ value of 2.71, the difference between the observed values and those of the model is *not* significant at the 10% level.

There is insufficient evidence (from the data) to conclude that ability to distinguish between margarine and butter is gender-related.

Exercise D (answers p. 84)

1   The following data compare performances of candidates in the sociology honours degree at two colleges.

			Grade		
	1	2	3	4	Total
College A	6	66	114	56	242
College B	5	40	86	49	180

Is there a significant difference in grades awarded?

2 In a hospital survey, staff were asked whether they were satisfied or
dissatisfied in their work. Results were as follows.

	Satisfied	Not satisfied	Total
Doctors	50	20	70
Nurses	30	30	60
Ancillary staff	12	48	60
Total	92	98	190

What evidence do these data provide that job satisfaction is related to
the type of job?

3 In a clinical trial of a drug for arthritis, 200 patients received treatment
with the drug, and a control group of 200 received treatment with a
seemingly identical placebo (which is non-active). After a period of
time, patients were asked if their condition had improved. The results
were as follows.

	Drug	Placebo
Improved	119	72
Not improved	81	128

Consider a chi-squared test to decide if these results give evidence
(significant at the 1% level) that the drug is effective in improving the
condition.

4 As part of the National Child Development Study, a report recorded
the numbers of boys and girls aged 7 who had had a temper tantrum
in the previous three months.

	Yes	No
Boys	1209	2849
Girls	1064	2863

Do these figures indicate a significant difference in behaviour between
boys and girls?

After working through this chapter you should

1 understand the difference between a deterministic and a probabilistic model and know when each is appropriate

2 understand the terms **observed** and **expected frequencies**, and be able to calculate expected frequencies from a probability model

3 be able to calculate the 'goodness of fit' statistic

$$X^2 = \sum_i \frac{(O_i - E_i)^2}{E_i}$$

4 know that the goodness of fit statistic X^2 has a distribution which can be modelled by one of the chi-squared functions

5 know the conditions under which the chi-squared test may be applied

6 know how to find areas under the chi-squared distribution using probability tables, and interpret these results in terms of probability

7 understand what is meant by **significance level** as applied to problems involving fitting probability models

8 be able to apply a chi-squared goodness of fit test to test probability models for data, including contingency tables

9 know how to work out the number of degrees of freedom by considering the number of constraints on the observed frequencies

10 know that an $m \times n$ contingency table has $(m-1)(n-1)$ degrees of freedom

11 be able to use Yates' correction for 2×2 contingency tables.

2 Probability distributions for counting cases

A The geometric distribution (answers p. 85)

Most people's lives follow a fairly routine pattern, although chance events do affect things. Nevertheless, an order emerges from the random events. Some of the emerging pattern may be modelled by random variables and the probability distributions which describe their behaviour.

For example, the number of girls in a family with four children is a random variable, X, which can take any of the values $X = 0, 1, 2, 3$ or 4. You should be aware that, with appropriate assumptions, X has a binomial probability distribution.

In Chapter 1 of *Statistics 1*, you considered the binomial distribution in some detail, and Chapter 3, 'The Normal distribution', was based entirely on one important probability distribution for a continuous random variable which is important for much of statistics.

All the distributions considered in this chapter apply to random variables which *count* events and therefore take whole-number values 0, 1, 2 and so on. The situations which they can be used to model will be compared and contrasted.

For example, on one day a midwife delivers eight boys in a row before the first girl is born. How rare is this event?

First you must clearly define a random variable. In this case, let X be the number of births *up to and including* the first girl; so X takes the values $\{1, 2, 3, ...\}$.

The random variable X does have a number of properties in common with a binomial variable. It is a discrete variable; there is a constant probability of the event occurring at each trial; and there is independence between trials. However, there is *not a fixed number of trials* (the value of n in the binomial distribution).

The probability distribution for X is considered below.

In Britain, it is slightly more likely that a baby is a boy. From census data, you can estimate the probability of a girl as 0.487 and of a boy as 0.513.

If you count the number of births until a girl is born, the possible events are G ($X = 1$), BG ($X = 2$), BBG ($X = 3$), BBBG, ... These can be illustrated by a tree diagram.

1 Draw a tree diagram to illustrate the outcomes. What assumptions do you need to make when drawing the tree diagram?

2 Use the tree diagram to write down the probability that the first female birth occurs at these occasions.

   (a) The first delivery (i.e. $X = 1$)

   (b) The second delivery (i.e. $X = 2$)

   (c) The fifth delivery ($X = 5$)

   (d) The nth delivery ($X = n$)

3 Use your answers to question 2 to complete the probability distribution for X, the number of children up to and including the first girl, for values of X up to 7. (Round the probabilities to 3 significant figures.)

4 Calculate the probability of seven or more boys being born before the first girl.

5 For a series of independent trials, let p be the probability that a chosen outcome occurs on any one particular trial. Let X be the number of trials needed to obtain the chosen outcome.

If $q = 1 - p$, show the following are true.

   (a) $P(X = 1) = p$

   (b) $P(X = 3) = q^2 p$

   (c) $P(X = n) = q^{n-1} p$

Notice that the sequence of probabilities $p, qp, q^2 p, q^3 p, \ldots$ forms a geometric series with common ratio q.

> If the random variable X counts the number of *independent trials* until the occurrence of an event whose probability is p, then X has a geometric distribution.
>
> The **geometric distribution**, abbreviated to G(p), is defined in the following way.
>
> $$P(X = r) = q^{r-1} p \quad \text{where } r = 1, 2, 3, \ldots$$

A cautionary note: you have been counting the number of trials up to and including the occurrence of the event itself, so that the lowest possible value of X is 1 (i.e. the event occurs at the first trial). Defined in this way, X cannot take the value 0. In some treatments of the geometric distribution, X is defined slightly differently, being the number of trials *before* the occurrence of the event. If X is defined in this way, its lowest possible value will be 0 (if the event occurs at the first trial, there are no trials before the occurrence).

Thus, you need to take care over how X is defined, both in the problems and exercises which follow, and elsewhere.

Example 1

To start a game of 'snakes and ladders', you need to throw a six.
Calculate the probability that it takes more than 6 throws to get a six.

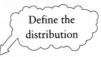

Define the distribution

Solution

Let X be the number of throws taken to get a six. Then $X \sim G(\frac{1}{6})$.

X takes the values $\{1, 2, 3, ...\}$.

$$P(X > 6) = 1 - P(X \leqslant 6)$$
$$= 1 - [P(X = 1) + ... + P(X = 6)]$$
$$= 1 - [\tfrac{1}{6} + (\tfrac{5}{6})\tfrac{1}{6} + (\tfrac{5}{6})^2\tfrac{1}{6} + ... + (\tfrac{5}{6})^5\tfrac{1}{6}]$$
$$= 0.335$$

The probability that it takes more than 6 throws is 0.335.

Alternatively,

$$P(6 \text{ 'non-sixes'}) = (\tfrac{5}{6})^6 = 0.335$$

The distribution of X is illustrated below.

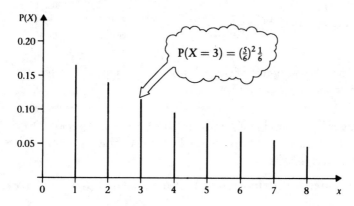

$P(X = 3) = (\tfrac{5}{6})^2\tfrac{1}{6}$

Exercise A (answers p. 85)

1   X has a geometric distribution with $p = 0.2$. Calculate the following.
   (a) $P(X = 3)$ (b) $P(X < 3)$ (c) $P(X \geqslant 3)$

2   I have a key ring on which there are four keys, all of the same type. To
   get into my office I select a key at random.
   (a) If it is a wrong key then I choose another at random from the
       remaining three. Calculate the probability that I try the following.
       (i)   Two keys
       (ii) All four keys

(b) If, instead, I simply keep choosing at random from all four keys until I get the correct one, calculate the probability that I try the following.

    (i) Two keys

    (ii) More than two keys

(c) Which strategy is better for getting into my office? Why?

3 Suppose that each time you take a driving test you have a probability of 0.4 of passing. What is the probability of these situations happening?

(a) You pass the test on the third attempt.

(b) You need at least six attempts to pass.

4 From a table of single-digit random numbers, what is the probability of these situations happening?

(a) You select five digits and you still do not have a zero.

(b) You need to select more than twenty digits to obtain your first zero.

B The binomial distribution revisited (answers p. 85)

On a particular morning, there are ten babies in the maternity ward at a local hospital. Only one of them is a boy. Just how likely an event is this?

1D	Identify the random variable in the situation described above and an appropriate binomial distribution to model it.

2D	Discuss the differences between the binomial and the geometric distributions by considering the conditions under which each applies.

To calculate binomial probabilities in Chapter 1 of *Statistics 1*, you used Pascal's triangle to work out $\binom{n}{r}$, the number of ways of choosing r objects from n. When n gets large, using Pascal's triangle is cumbersome. Even though you can use the Normal approximation to the binomial when n is large, the following formula for evaluating $\binom{n}{r}$ is useful.

$$\binom{n}{r} = \frac{n!}{r!(n-r)!} \qquad \text{where} \quad n! = n(n-1)(n-2) \ldots 1$$
$$\text{and} \qquad 0! = 1$$

The number $\binom{n}{r}$ is sometimes written as ^nC_r or $_nC_r$.

If $X \sim B(n, p)$, then:

$$P(X = r) = \binom{n}{r} p^r q^{n-r} \qquad r = 0, 1, 2, \ldots, n$$

$$P(X = r) = \frac{n!}{r!(n-r)!} p^r q^{n-r}$$

3   Use the factorial form of the binomial distribution to find the probability of there being only one male baby in a group of ten.

Example 2

Approximately 20% of the pupils at a primary school are vegetarians. Seven of the pupils are to visit another school and have lunch there. Calculate the probability that, in addition to normal requirements, the school will need to provide the following.

(a) Three vegetarian lunches   (b) At least one vegetarian lunch

Solution

Specify the random variable

Let X be the number of vegetarians on the visit.
$$X \sim B(7, 0.20)$$

Specify its probability distribution

(a) $P(X = 3) = \binom{7}{3}(0.2)^3(0.8)^4 = \left(\frac{7!}{3!4!}\right)(0.2)^3(0.8)^4$

$= 0.115$ $= 35$

(b) $P(X \geqslant 1) = 1 - P(X = 0) = 1 - 0.8^7 = 0.79$

4E   Using the factorial formula for $P(X = r)$, show that

$$P(X = r+1) = \left(\frac{n-r}{r+1}\right)\frac{p}{q} P(X = r)$$

5   Use the result in question 4E to calculate the following probability distributions.

(a) $B(3, \frac{1}{4})$ (b) $B(4, \frac{1}{3})$

Exercise B (answers p. 86)

1 In a series of five matches between two teams, calculate the probability that one team wins the toss on these occasions.

(a) Exactly three   (b) Three or more

2 If $X \sim B(8, \frac{2}{3})$, find the most likely value of X.

3 Six people, selected at random, sample two brands of orange squash, brands A and B. If five of them say they prefer brand B, do you think this is sufficient evidence for an advertiser to say, 'Most people prefer brand B'? Explain.

4 In a multiple-choice test where there are only three possible answers to each of the twenty questions, a student randomly guesses each answer. If fifteen is the pass mark for the test, calculate the probability that he passes.

5E A coin is tossed eight times. What is the probability that there will be more tails on the first four throws than on the last four?

C **The Poisson distribution** (answers p. 87)

A small company handles emergency medical deliveries by motorcycle. On average, it receives four delivery requests in a 12-hour period. When it gets more than four emergency requests, it has to pass on the work to another company. The company wishes to know the probability of this happening to enable it to evaluate its employment policy.

Let X be the number of emergency calls in a 12-hour period.

> **1D** What values can X take? Could the distribution of X be binomial, or geometric? What sort of shape do you think the graph of the distribution will take?

It is possible to find *approximate* binomial models which describe the demands on the emergency system.

To use the binomial model we must assume that delivery requests are independent, i.e. if a request is received in one period it is no more or less likely that a request will be received in a subsequent period.

On average, requests for deliveries are made four times in a 12-hour period. Assume that in each hour no more than one request can be made. So for each hour,

$$P(\text{request}) = \frac{1}{3}$$
$$P(\text{no request}) = \frac{2}{3}$$

and the total number of requests in 12 hours will be $B(12, \frac{1}{3})$.

2 (a) Show that this model has the correct mean.

   (b) Complete the probability distribution of X.

X	0	1	2	3	4	5	6	7	8	9	10	11	12
$P(X=x)$	?	0.046	0.127	0.212	?	0.191	0.111	0.048	?	0.003	0	0	0

This model is not very realistic since there could be more than one request in any one hour. Suppose you assumed that no more than one request is made in each 15-minute interval.

3 (a) For any 15-minute interval, calculate P(request).

   (b) Define a binomial distribution of X using the assumption that no more than one request is made in each 15-minute interval.

   (c) Calculate the probabilities $P(X=x)$ for values of x up to 12 and compare them with your answer to question 2.

There could still be more than one request made in a 15-minute interval, although this is less likely than when intervals of an hour are considered. Suppose you consider one-minute intervals.

4 Given that no more than one request is made in any one minute, find a binomial model for X. Calculate $P(X=x)$ for $x \leqslant 12$.

5 Repeat question 4 using intervals of 6 seconds.

You could continue this process of considering smaller and smaller intervals of time and assuming at most one event in each interval. The smaller the interval you choose, the more realistic will be the binomial model obtained.

This is equivalent to taking a series of binomial distributions B(n, p), where the mean np is constant (equal to 4) but n increases and p decreases. The probabilities associated with each of the distributions you have defined for X are summarised in the table.

X	B($12, \frac{1}{3}$)	B($48, \frac{1}{12}$)	B($720, \frac{1}{180}$)	B($7200, \frac{1}{1800}$)
0	0.008	0.015	0.018	0.018
1	0.046	0.067	0.073	0.073
2	0.127	0.143	0.146	0.147
3	0.212	0.199	0.196	0.195
4	0.238	0.204	0.196	0.195
5	0.191	0.163	0.157	0.156
6	0.111	0.106	0.104	0.104
7	0.048	0.058	0.060	0.060
8	0.015	0.027	0.030	0.030
9	0.003	0.011	0.013	0.013
10	0.000	0.004	0.005	0.005

From the table, you can see that these distributions seem to tend to a limiting distribution, which can be assumed to be the true distribution of X.

6 For each distribution, show that $np = 4$.

The correct probability distribution for X, for which the binomial models above are approximations, is given by the formula

$$P(X = r) = \frac{e^{-4}4^r}{r!}$$

7 What is the significance of the 4 in this expression?

This result is justified in Section D below.

8 Confirm that this formula gives the same probability distribution (to 3 s.f.) as $B(7200, \frac{1}{1800})$ above.

9 Calculate the probability of four or more requests using the probability distribution

$$P(X = r) = \frac{e^{-4}4^r}{r!} \quad \text{where } r = 0, 1, 2, 3, \ldots$$

This probability distribution is called the **Poisson distribution**, after the French statistician, Siméon Denis Poisson (1781–1840).

X is said to have a **Poisson distribution** with mean λ if

$$P(X = r) = \frac{e^{-\lambda}\lambda^r}{r!} \quad \text{for } r = 0, 1, 2, 3, \ldots$$

This is written as

$$X \sim P(\lambda)$$

(λ is the Greek letter l, pronounced 'lambda'.)

Poisson derived his probability distribution by considering what happens to the binomial distribution when n increases and np is kept fixed.

The mean of the binomial distribution $B(n, p)$ is np. As it is np that determines the particular Poisson distribution $P(\lambda)$, then it is likely that λ will be the mean of the Poisson. This result will be proved in Chapter 5 Section D, where the means of various distributions are considered.

Example 3

Cars arrive at a petrol station at an average rate of two cars every 10 minutes. For a given 10-minute period, calculate these probabilities.

(a) Exactly three cars arrive   (b) Two or more cars arrive

Solution

(a) Let X be the number of cars arriving in a 10-minute period.

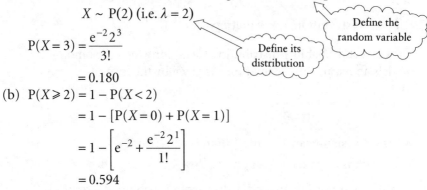

$$X \sim P(2) \text{ (i.e. } \lambda = 2)$$

$$P(X = 3) = \frac{e^{-2}2^3}{3!}$$

$$= 0.180$$

(b) $P(X \geqslant 2) = 1 - P(X < 2)$

$$= 1 - [P(X = 0) + P(X = 1)]$$

$$= 1 - \left[e^{-2} + \frac{e^{-2}2^1}{1!} \right]$$

$$= 0.594$$

Using the Poisson distribution as an approximation to the binomial distribution

For large values of n, calculations of probabilities using the binomial distribution can be tedious.

You have seen how, as n gets large but np remains constant, the binomial distribution $B(n, p)$ tends to the Poisson distribution $P(np)$.

For large n and small p, this allows us to use the Poisson distribution as an approximation to the binomial distribution.

> If n is large (> 50) and p is small (< 0.1), the binomial distribution $B(n, p)$ can be approximated by the Poisson distribution $P(np)$.

Example 4

In a card game, a player is dealt four cards from a pack of fifty-two cards of which thirteen are spades. A winning hand consists of four spades.

(a) Calculate the probability that a player will receive a winning hand.

(b) Using the Poisson distribution as an approximation to the binomial distribution, calculate the probability that a player does not receive a winning hand if he plays the game 50 times.

(c) Calculate the probability of a player winning three or more hands if he plays the game 500 times.

Solution

(a) P(player receives 4 spades) $= \frac{13}{52} \times \frac{12}{51} \times \frac{11}{50} \times \frac{10}{49} = 0.002\ 64$

(b) P(no winning hand in 50 games)

$$= \frac{e^{-\lambda}\lambda^0}{0!} \text{ where } \lambda = np = 50 \times 0.002\ 64$$
$$= 0.876$$

(c) P(3 or more winning hands in 500 games)

$$= 1 - e^{-\lambda} - e^{-\lambda}\lambda - \frac{e^{-\lambda}\lambda^2}{2!} \text{ where } \lambda = np = 500 \times 0.002\ 64$$
$$= 0.148$$

Exercise C (answers p. 87)

1 On average, 2% of goods on a production line are found to be defective. A random sample of 100 items is taken from production.

(a) What is the mean number of defective goods in a sample of 100?

(b) Use a suitable binomial model to find the probability of these.

    (i)   No defective items in the batch

    (ii) At least one defective item in the batch

(c) Repeat the calculations in (b) using the Poisson distribution to approximate the binomial probabilities.

2 If $X \sim P(5)$, calculate these.

(a) $P(X = 0)$ (b) $P(X = 2)$ (c) $P(X \geqslant 2)$

3 Over a period of time it was shown that a particular daily paper had on average 1.4 misprints per page.

Calculate these.

(a) The probability of finding no misprints on a page

(b) The probability of finding a page with two or more misprints

4 On average, customers arrive at a supermarket check-out till at the rate of 2.4 per minute. A queue begins to develop if more than three people arrive in a given minute. Use a Poisson model to find the probability that a queue develops.

5 A Geiger counter records alpha-particles striking a sensor. If the average rate is 0.6 particles a second, calculate the probabilities of 0, 1, 2 and 3 or more particles striking the sensor within a one-second interval.

6 Cars travelling randomly along a road at an average rate of two a minute arrive at a level crossing. If the crossing gates are closed for a minute to allow a train to pass, what is the probability that more than two cars will be held up?

7 On average I get 30 letters a week (Monday to Saturday). Would you expect a Poisson probability model to be a suitable way of finding the probabilities of getting various numbers of letters in each day's mail? On this assumption, calculate the probability that on a particular day I shall receive fewer than three letters.

8 Telephone calls coming in to a switchboard follow a Poisson probability model with an average rate of three a minute. Find the probability that in a given minute there will be five or more calls.

D From binomial to Poisson (answers p. 88)

You have seen that the binomial distribution $N(n, p)$ appears to 'tend to' the Poisson distribution $P(\lambda)$, when

$$\lambda = np \quad \text{and} \quad n \to \infty$$

As a mathematician you will want to know why!

You have shown that, for a binomial random variable,

$$P(X = r+1) = \left(\frac{n-r}{r+1}\right)\frac{p}{q} P(X = r) \quad \text{and} \quad P(X = 0) = q^n$$

1E For a Poisson random variable, show that

$$P(X = r+1) = \frac{\lambda}{r+1} P(X = r) \quad \text{and} \quad P(X = 0) = e^{-\lambda}$$

You now need to show that as $n \to \infty$ and $p \to 0$, with $np = \lambda$,

$$q^n \to e^{-\lambda} \tag{1}$$

$$\left(\frac{n-r}{r+1}\right)\frac{p}{q} \to \frac{\lambda}{r+1} \tag{2}$$

The Maclaurin series for e^x is

$$e^x = 1 + \frac{x}{1!} + \frac{x^2}{2!} + \frac{x^3}{3!} + \dots$$

2E Write down the Maclaurin series for $e^{-\lambda}$.

3E Show that

$$q^n = \left(1 - \frac{\lambda}{n}\right)^n$$

Find the first four terms of the binomial expansion.

4E Deduce that as $n \to \infty$, $q^n \to e^{-\lambda}$. This demonstrates equation (1).

5E To demonstrate equation (2), show that

$$\frac{(n-r)p}{q} = \frac{\left(1 - \dfrac{r}{n}\right)}{\left(1 - \dfrac{\lambda}{n}\right)} \lambda$$

Deduce that as $n \to \infty$, $\dfrac{(n-r)p}{q} \to \lambda$ and hence

$$\frac{(n-r)}{(r+1)} \frac{p}{q} \to \frac{\lambda}{r+1}$$

After working through this chapter you should

1 be familiar with the geometric, binomial and Poisson distributions and the situations they describe

2 be able to calculate the probabilities of events described by these distributions.

3 Continuous random variables

A The Normal probability density function (answers p. 88)

So far this book has concentrated on *discrete* random variables and some important probability models associated with them. There are, of course, models for *continuous* random variables, the single most important being the Normal probability model which you considered in Chapter 3 of *Statistics 1*. It is worth looking at an example as a reminder before considering other continuous probability distributions.

1D A machine is set to deliver sugar into bags. The weight of sugar it delivers is Normally distributed, having a mean of 1.1 kg and standard deviation 0.1 kg.
(a) Approximately what proportion of bags marked 1 kg will be underweight?
(b) Confirm your answer to (a) by calculating this proportion using Normal tables (page 102).

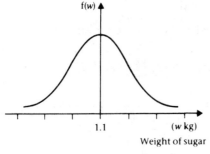

The graph of this distribution is called the **Normal probability density function**.

If X is any continuous random variable, the probability that X takes a value between a and b is given by the area under the probability density function for X, between $X = a$ and $X = b$. This area is usually calculated by direct integration in the case of simple functions, or by using tables which give the area in the two important cases of the Normal and chi-squared distributions (see pages 102 and 103).

$$P(a \leqslant X \leqslant b) = \int_a^b f(x)\, dx$$

Example 1

A certain manufacturer claims that there are 64 g of real fruit in every 100 g of their jam. The actual weight of fruit in the jam is distributed Normally, having a mean weight of 68 g and standard deviation 1.6 g. Calculate the proportion of 100 g measures of jam which contain the following.

(a) More than 70 g of fruit

(b) Less than 64 g of fruit

Solution

Let the weight of fruit in 100 g of jam be W g. Then $W \sim N(68, 1.6^2)$.

(a)

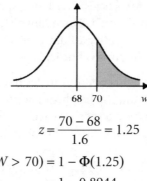

$$z = \frac{70 - 68}{1.6} = 1.25$$

$$P(W > 70) = 1 - \Phi(1.25)$$
$$= 1 - 0.8944$$
$$= 0.106 \text{ (to 3 s.f.)}$$

So 10.6% of the 100 g measures will contain more than 70 g of fruit.

(b)

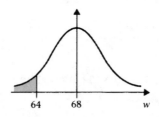

$$z = \frac{64 - 68}{1.6} = -2.5$$

$$P(W < 64) = \Phi(-2.5)$$
$$= 1 - \Phi(2.5)$$
$$= 0.006$$

So 0.6% of the 100 g measures will contain less than 64 g of fruit.

Exercise A (answers p. 89)

1 My journey to work takes 20 minutes on average, with a standard deviation of 5 minutes. The journey time may be considered to be Normally distributed. If I take longer than 26 minutes, I am late. Calculate the probability of my being late.

2 The length of time that a particular make of light bulb lasts is distributed Normally, having mean 2000 hours and standard deviation 50 hours. Calculate the probability that a particular light bulb will last these lengths of time.

(a) Longer than 1970 hours

(b) Between 2050 and 2080 hours.

3 The mean survival period for daisies after being sprayed with a weed killer is 20 days. The survival time is Normally distributed. If a quarter of the daisies are still surviving after 23 days, calculate an estimate for the standard deviation of the survival time.

4 In a certain country, the heights of adult males have mean 170 cm and standard deviation 10 cm, and the heights of adult females have mean 160 cm and standard deviation 8 cm; for each sex the distribution of heights approximates closely to a Normal probability model. On the hypothesis that height is not a factor in selecting a mate, calculate the probability that a husband and wife selected at random are both taller than 164 cm.

B General probability density functions (answers p. 89)

A general probability density function $f(x)$ must have the following properties.

> - $f(x) \geqslant 0$ for all x
> - The total area under the curve $f(x)$ must be 1 .

1D | Explain why $f(x)$ must have these properties.

Example 2

A probability density function $f(x)$ is defined as follows.

$$f(x) = \begin{cases} \dfrac{k}{x^2} & \text{for } 1 \leqslant x \leqslant 6 \\ 0 & \text{for all other } x \end{cases}$$

Find the value of k.

Solution

$$\int_1^6 f(x)\,dx = 1, \quad \text{so} \quad \int_1^6 \frac{k}{x^2}\,dx = 1$$

$$\Rightarrow \int_1^6 \frac{1}{x^2}\,dx = 1$$

$$\Rightarrow \left[-\frac{1}{x}\right]_1^6 = 1$$

$$\Rightarrow k[(-\tfrac{1}{6}) - (-\tfrac{1}{1})] = 1$$

$$\Rightarrow \tfrac{5}{6}\,k = 1$$

$$\Rightarrow k = \tfrac{6}{5} = 1.2$$

Example 3

The incubation period, X days, for a particular infection is modelled by the probability density function $f(x)$, where $f(x)$ is defined as

$$f(x) = \tfrac{1}{144}(36 - x^2) \qquad \text{for } 0 \leqslant x \leqslant 6$$

What is the probability that you will show symptoms of the infection during the second day?

Solution

$$P(1 \leqslant X \leqslant 2) = \int_1^2 f(x)\,dx$$

$$= \int_1^2 \tfrac{1}{144}(36 - x^2)\,dx$$

$$= \tfrac{1}{144}[36x - \tfrac{1}{3}x^3]_1^2$$

$$= \tfrac{1}{144}[(72 - \tfrac{8}{3}) - (36 - \tfrac{1}{3})]$$

$$= 0.23 \qquad \text{(to 2 s.f.)}$$

The probability that you will show symptoms on the second day is 0.23.

2 What is the probability of showing symptoms on the first day?

Exercise B (answers p. 89)

In each of the questions f(x) refers to a probability density function.

1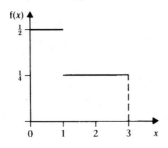

(a) Define the possible values of X.

(b) Show that the area under the graph of $f(x)$ is 1.

(c) Find these.

  (i) $P(X \geqslant 1)$

  (ii) $P(X \geqslant \frac{1}{2})$

  (iii) $P(\frac{1}{2} \leqslant X \leqslant 2)$

  (iv) $P(X \leqslant 3)$

2 (a) Find k.

  (b) Find these.

  (i) $P(X \geqslant 1.5)$

  (ii) $P(X \leqslant 0.5)$

  (iii) $P(0.5 \leqslant X \leqslant 1.5)$

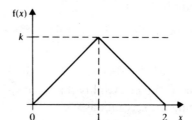

3 In a game, a wooden block is propelled with a stick across a flat deck. On each attempt, the distance, X metres, travelled by the block lies between 0 and 10 metres, and the distribution of the distances is given by the probability density function

$$f(x) = 0.0012x^2(10 - x)$$

Calculate the probability that the block travels these distances.

(a) More than 5 metres

(b) Between 1 and 2 metres

C Cumulative distribution functions (answers p. 90)

We can define a function, $F(x)$ for the continuous random variable X, as the function that gives the probability that X takes a value below x.

You have already met such a function, $\Phi(z)$ for the standardised Normal distribution.

As a special case of the result $P(a < X < b) = \int_a^b f(x)\, dx$ for continuous random variables, we will consider only the probability that the variable takes a value less than t. There is no lower limit, a.

$$P(X < t) = P(-\infty < X < t) = \int_{-\infty}^{t} f(x)\, dx$$

We define $F(t) = \int_{-\infty}^{t} f(x)\,dx$ and call it the **cumulative distribution function** of X.

The cumulative distribution function can be used in place of the probability density function to find the probability that the variable lies within a certain range.

$$P(a < X < b) = \int_{a}^{b} f(x)\,dx$$

$$= \int_{-\infty}^{b} f(x)\,dx - \int_{-\infty}^{a} f(x)\,dx$$

$$= F(b) - F(a)$$

The fundamental theorem of calculus (*Methods*, page 105) states that for any differentiable function g

$$\int_{a}^{b} g'(x)\,dx = g(b) - g(a)$$

Applying this theorem to the cumulative distribution function $F(x)$,

$$\int_{a}^{b} F'(x)\,dx = F(b) - F(a)$$

But we have already seen that by our definition of $F(x)$,

$$\int_{a}^{b} f(x)\,dx = F(b) - F(a)$$

where $f(x)$ is the probability density function for the distribution. Therefore we can see that

$$F'(x) = f(x)$$

Where a distribution has cumulative distribution function $F(x)$ and probability density function $f(x)$

$$f(x) = \frac{d}{dx} F(x)$$

Exercise C (answers p. 90)

1   A distribution has probability density function $f(x)$ defined as follows.

$$f(x) = \begin{cases} k & \text{for } a \leqslant x \leqslant b \\ 0 & \text{for all other } x \end{cases}$$

(a) Find the value of k.

(b) Find the cumulative distribution function $F(x)$ for the distribution.

2 The probability that an event will occur during a time interval of
   t seconds is given by

$$P \text{ (event occurs during time } t) = F(t) = \begin{cases} 0 & \text{for } t < 1 \\ 1 - \dfrac{1}{t} & \text{for } t \geqslant 1 \end{cases}$$

(a) Find the probability that the event occurs within 5 seconds.
(b) Find the probability that the event occurs after 2 seconds but
     within 4 seconds.
(c) What is the probability density function $f(t)$ for the timing of the
     event?

D The mean, variance and other measures of variability
(answers p. 90)

For a discrete variable X, the mean μ was defined by

$$\mu = \sum_i x_i P(x_i)$$

The analogous form of this definition for a continuous variable X
having probability density function $f(x)$ is

$$\mu = \int x f(x) \, dx \qquad \text{where the integral is taken over the whole range of } X \text{ values.}$$

For the variance, the expression equivalent to

$$\sigma^2 = \sum_i x_i^2 P(x_i) - \mu^2 \qquad \text{(for a discrete variable)}$$

is

$$\sigma^2 = \int x^2 f(x) \, dx - \mu^2 \qquad \text{(for a continuous variable)}$$

and the standard deviation will therefore be

$$\sigma = \sqrt{\int x^2 f(x) \, dx - \mu^2}$$

If X is a continuous random variable having a probability density
function $f(x)$ when $a \leqslant x \leqslant b$,

$$\mu = \int_a^b x f(x) \, dx$$

$$\sigma^2 = \int_a^b x^2 f(x) \, dx - \mu^2$$

$$\sigma = \sqrt{\int_a^b x^2 f(x) \, dx - \mu^2}$$

Example 4

A probability density function $f(x)$ is defined as follows.

$$f(x) = \begin{cases} ke^{2x} & \text{for } 0 \leqslant x \leqslant 1 \\ 0 & \text{otherwise} \end{cases}$$

(a) Find k.
(b) Calculate the mean value of x.
(c) Calculate the median value of x.

Solution

(a) $k\displaystyle\int_0^1 e^{2x}\,dx = 1 \implies k\left[\dfrac{e^{2x}}{2}\right]_0^1 = 1$

$$k\left(\frac{e^2}{2} - \frac{1}{2}\right) = 1$$

$$k = \frac{2}{e^2 - 1} = 0.313 \quad \text{(to 3 s.f.)}$$

(b) $\mu = \displaystyle\int_0^1 x\,f(x)\,dx = k\int_0^1 xe^{2x}\,dx$

$$= k\left[\frac{xe^{2x}}{2} - \int \frac{e^{2x}}{2}\,dx\right]_0^1 \qquad \text{using integration by parts}$$

$$= k\left[\frac{xe^{2x}}{2} - \frac{e^{2x}}{4}\right]_0^1$$

$$= 0.657 \quad \text{(to 3 s.f.)}$$

(c) If the median is m then $\displaystyle\int_0^m f(x)\,dx = 0.5$

$$k\int_0^m e^{2x}\,dx = 0.5$$

$$\left[\frac{e^{2x}}{2}\right]_0^m = \frac{0.5}{k}$$

$$\frac{e^{2m}}{2} - \frac{1}{2} = \frac{0.5}{k}$$

$$e^{2m} = 4.195$$

$$2m = \ln 4.195$$

$$m = 0.717 \quad \text{(to 3 s.f.)}$$

The area under the graph of $f(x)$ is divided in half by the vertical through $x = m$.

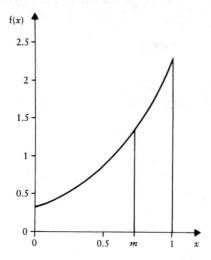

The result established above can be written using the cumulative distribution function as

$$F(m) = 0.5$$

We can similarly divide the area under the graph of $f(x)$ into quarters by the verticals through $x = q_1$, the lower quartile, and $x = q_3$ the upper quartile.

Percentiles are also used to describe populations. The weights of babies in their first few weeks are sometimes recorded on graphs which show the 5th and 95th percentiles for the whole population. Ninety per cent of babies will have weights within these limits.

Example 5

A continuous random variable has probability density function

$$f(x) = \begin{cases} \dfrac{1}{50}(10 - x) & \text{for } 0 \leqslant x \leqslant 10 \\ 0 & \text{otherwise} \end{cases}$$

Calculate the mean, median, lower quartile and 95th percentile for the variable.

Solution

The mean, $\mu = \dfrac{1}{50} \displaystyle\int_0^{10} x(10 - x)\, dx$

$$= \tfrac{1}{50}[5x^2 - \tfrac{1}{3}x^3]_0^{10}$$
$$= 3.33 \quad \text{(to 3 s.f.)}$$

The median, lower quartile and 95th percentile can be found using $F(m) = 0.5$, $F(q_1) = 0.25$ and $F(p) = 0.95$.

$$\frac{dF(x)}{dx} = f(x) = \tfrac{1}{50}(10 - x) \quad \text{for } 0 \leqslant x \leqslant 10$$

Therefore $F(x) = \tfrac{1}{50}\left(10x - \tfrac{1}{2}x^2\right) = \tfrac{1}{100}\left(20x - x^2\right)$ for $0 \leqslant x \leqslant 10$.

If m is the median

$$F(m) = \tfrac{1}{100}(20m - m^2) = 0.5$$

$$20m - m^2 = 50$$

$$m = 2.93 \quad \text{(to 3 s.f.)}$$

If q_1 is the lower quartile

$$F(q_1) = \tfrac{1}{100}(20q_1 - q_1^2) = 0.25$$

$$20q_1 - q_1^2 = 25$$

$$q_1 = 1.34 \quad \text{(to 3 s.f.)}$$

If p is the 95th percentile

$$F(p) = \tfrac{1}{100}(20p - p^2) = 0.95$$

$$20p - p^2 = 95$$

$$p = 7.76 \quad \text{(to 3 s.f.)}$$

Exercise D (answers p. 90)

1 A random variable X has probability density function $f(x)$, where

$$f(x) = \begin{cases} kx^2 & 0 \leqslant x \leqslant 1 \\ 0 & \text{otherwise} \end{cases}$$

(a) Show that $k = 3$.

(b) Calculate the mean and variance of X.

(c) Find the probability that $X \geqslant 0.5$.

2 A department store will deliver parcels within a range of 5 to 15 miles. The probability of a delivery being for a distance X miles is given by the probability density function $f(x)$, where

$$f(x) = \begin{cases} \dfrac{k}{x^3} & 5 \leqslant x \leqslant 15 \\ 0 & \text{otherwise} \end{cases}$$

(a) Calculate k and sketch a graph of $f(x)$.

(b) Find the mean delivery distance.

(c) Half of all deliveries are for distances of m miles or more. Find m.

3   The distance (X metres) travelled by a wooden block in a game is given by the probability density function $f(x)$, where

$$f(x) = \begin{cases} 0.0012x^2(10-x) & 0 \leqslant x \leqslant 10 \\ 0 & \text{otherwise} \end{cases}$$

Calculate the mean distance travelled.

4   A random variable X has a probability density function $f(x)$, where

$$f(x) = \begin{cases} \dfrac{k}{1+x} & \text{for } 1 \leqslant x \leqslant 2 \\ 0 & \text{otherwise} \end{cases}$$

(a) Show that $k = \dfrac{1}{\ln \frac{3}{2}}$.

(b) Find the median value of X.

(c) Find $P(X > 1.5)$.

5   A random variable X has a probability density function $f(x)$ defined as follows.

$$f(x) = \begin{cases} kx(x-1) & \text{for } 0 \leqslant x \leqslant 1 \\ 0 & \text{otherwise} \end{cases}$$

(a) Find k.

(b) Sketch the graph of $f(x)$. Explain why the median value of x is 0.5.

(c) Find $P(X > 0.75)$.

6   A random variable has cumulative distribution function,

$$F(x) = \begin{cases} 0 & x < 0 \\ 0.25x & 0 \leqslant x < 1 \\ 0.5(x-0.5) & 1 \leqslant x < 1 \\ 0.25(x+1) & 2 \leqslant x < 3 \\ 1 & 3 \leqslant x \end{cases}$$

Find the probability density function $f(x)$ of X, and the 5th and 95th percentiles of the distribution.

After working through this chapter you should

1 know what probability density means for a continuous random variable

2 know how to calculate the mean, variance and standard deviation from a probability density function

3 know how to calculate the probability of an event when given the probability density function of the variable

4 know and understand that, if $f(x)$ is a probability density function, then

(a) $f(x) \geqslant 0$ for all x

(b) $\int f(x) \, dx = 1$

5 know how the probability density function and cumulative distribution function are related.

4 Selecting and testing the models

A Choosing a suitable model (answers p. 91)

A basketball player counts the number of shots he takes to score a basket. He records the following data.

Shots taken	Frequency
1	14
2	11
3	7
4	6
5	3
6	2
7	0
8	1

1D
> (a) Of the models you have considered for counting cases (Chapter 2), which do you think is the most suitable here? Consider carefully the reasons for your choice.
>
> (b) What assumptions need to be made for your chosen model to be suitable?

2 For each of these variables, suggest whether the binomial, Poisson or geometric is likely to be a suitable model. State assumptions you need to make and define the model where possible.

(a) The number of sixes obtained when five dice are thrown.

(b) The number of throws needed until you obtain a six on a dice.

(c) The number of boys in families of four children.

(d) The number of clicks made by a geiger counter in a five-second interval.

(e) The number of home matches a team plays until they score a goal.

Exercise A (answers p. 91)

1 A survey of 300 families with five children produced the following
results for the number of boys (X) in the family.

Number of boys (X)	Number of families
0	7
1	37
2	82
3	104
4	54
5	16
Total	300

(a) Explain why these data might be modelled by a binomial
distribution and state the assumptions necessary to use
$X \sim B(5, \frac{1}{2})$ as a model.

(b) Use the chi-squared distribution to test $X \sim B(5, \frac{1}{2})$.

(c) Use the data to estimate p, the probability of a male birth, and test
$X \sim B(5, p)$. Take care over the number of degrees of freedom for
the χ^2 test.

(d) Which of the two models best fits this data set? Give a reason for
your choice.

2 Four drawing pins are thrown into the air and the number (N) landing
point up is counted.

(a) Explain why N has a binomial distribution.

The four pins are thrown 300 times with the following results.

Number landing point up (N)	Frequency
0	10
1	48
2	120
3	86
4	36

(b) (i) Calculate the mean number landing point up and hence
obtain an estimate of p, the probability that a pin lands point
up.

(ii) Use the χ^2 test to assess the suitability of $N \sim B(4, p)$ as a
model for the data.

B The geometric distribution as a model (answers p. 92)

You may have considered the geometric distribution as a suitable model for the basketball data.

Shots taken	Frequency
1	14
2	11
3	7
4	6
5	3
6	2
7	0
8	1

The geometric distribution, $G(p)$, depends only on the probability p of the event. Since you have no prior information on which to base a value for p, it must be obtained from the data. Remember that this provides a *constraint* which reduces the number of degrees of freedom by one when you conduct the χ^2 test.

> Set up a model

The data show that the player scored 44 baskets out of 116 shots.

An estimate of the probability of scoring a basket is

$$P(\text{scoring a basket}) = \tfrac{44}{116}$$
$$= 0.379$$

Suppose that $X \sim G(0.379)$ where X is the number of shots needed to score a basket.

The probability distribution and expected frequencies are as follows.

x	$P(x)$	Expected frequency
1	0.379	16.7
2	0.235	10.4
3	0.146	6.4
4	0.091	4.0
5	0.056	2.5
6	0.035	1.5
7	0.022	1.0
$\geqslant 8$	0.036	1.6

Analyse the problem

To apply a chi-squared test, you need to ensure that the cells have *expected frequencies of at least five* to ensure that X^2 has approximately a χ^2 distribution. You can do this by combining the cells as indicated to obtain the following.

x	Observed frequencies	Expected frequencies
1	14	16.7
2	11	10.4
3	7	6.4
4 or more	12	10.6

$$X^2 = \sum \frac{(O-E)^2}{E} = \frac{(14-16.7)^2}{16.7} + \frac{(11-10.4)^2}{10.4} + ...$$

$$X^2 = 0.71 \quad \text{(to 2 s.f.)}$$

There are four cells on which the calculation of X^2 is based. However, there are *two* constraints – the total number of baskets must be 44, and the probability ($p = 0.379$) has been estimated from the data. There are therefore $4 - 2 = 2$ degrees of freedom.

Testing X^2 with two degrees of freedom, $X^2 > 5.99$ in 5% of samples (from tables). Since $0.71 < 5.99$, the proposed model is not rejected at the 5% level.

Interpret/validate

The geometric distribution with $p = 0.379$ is a reasonably good model for the data given.

The activity that follows is a data collection exercise in which you consider two different geometric models as possible models for the data.

You will need a calculator or tables for obtaining random numbers.

Random digits (0, 1, 2, ..., 9) are produced so that each has an equal probability of occurrence. Count the number of digits that occur up to the occurrence of the first zero. This is called the **run length**.

1, 3, 9, 7, 0	five digits needed to get zero
3, 6, 0	three digits needed
0	one digit needed

1 Use your random number generator and count the digits generated up to and including the first zero. Repeat about 200 times and complete the table.

Length of run (L)	1	2	3	4	...
Number of runs					

2 State the assumptions necessary to use $L \sim G(\frac{1}{10})$ as a model here. Why does $p = \frac{1}{10}$?

3 Set up and test the $G(\frac{1}{10})$ model against your data. Take care to combine groups as necessary when using the χ^2 test. This, of course, has an effect on the number of degrees of freedom for the test.

4 Use the data to calculate an estimate of p, where p is the probability of obtaining a run of length one.

5 Set up and test an alternative model $G(p)$. Which of the two models is better for your data? Why?

6 Calculate the mean run length for your data.

C Fitting a Poisson distribution to data (answers p. 92)

There are many situations where you can identify an event which is occurring randomly and independently in time (or space), but with a fixed average number of occurrences per unit interval of time (or space).

Randomly occurring event	Unit of time or space
A case of appendicitis is diagnosed	A day in hospital
A geiger counter clicks	A 5-second interval
A telephone rings	A 15-minute interval
A water flea is found	A jar of pond water

Examples of this kind are called **Poisson processes**, and in so far as they fit the conditions above, they can be modelled effectively by the Poisson distribution.

Example 1

After a nuclear accident, the number of cases of thyroid disease in babies born in the vicinity was eleven. The average for an equivalent period in the same vicinity was three. Model the situation with a Poisson distribution, stating the assumptions behind the model. Does this provide evidence that the nuclear accident increased the risk of thyroid disease?

Solution

Let X be the number of occurrences of thyroid disease in babies.
Then X is a Poisson variable with mean 3, assuming that:

- the same vicinity and length of period are considered
- thyroid disease occurs randomly in babies
- incidences of thyroid disease in babies occur independently.

On the basis of the model,

$$P(X \geqslant 11) = 1 - P(X \leqslant 10)$$
$$P(X \leqslant 10) = P(0) + P(1) + ... + P(10)$$

$$= e^{-3} + 3e^{-3} + \frac{3^2 e^{-3}}{2!} + ... + \frac{3^{10} e^{-3}}{10!}$$

$$= 0.9997$$
$$\Rightarrow \quad P(X \geqslant 11) = 0.0003$$

It is therefore extremely unlikely that this number of cases of thyroid disease in babies would have occurred by chance.

Of course, this in itself does not prove that the nuclear accident caused the increase in thyroid disease in babies – there may have been other factors present. However, it does suggest that a possible connection is worth further investigation.

A Poisson distribution is defined in terms of its mean, λ, and you will prove later (Chapter 5, Section D) that the variance of a Poisson distribution is equal to its mean. By comparing the mean and variance of a set of data, you can check whether a Poisson model for the data is reasonable.

Exercise C (answers p. 92)

1   The numbers of people arriving at a post office queue in each of 60 consecutive one-minute intervals are summarised in the table.

Number of arrivals (X)	0	1	2	3	4	5
Number of one minutes (f)	15	19	19	5	1	1

   (a) Calculate the mean and variance of the number of people arriving in a one-minute interval.

   (b) Explain why the Poisson model might be considered a suitable model for the data.

2   Pityriasis rosea is a skin disorder which has never been shown to be infectious. The number of cases reported in each of 100 consecutive weeks in a particular town was recorded. The data are summarised in the table.

Number of cases (X)	0	1	2	3	4	5	6	7
Number of weeks (f)	31	34	22	8	3	1	0	1

(a) Justify the use of a Poisson model for these data.

(b) Obtain the 'expected' frequencies based on a suitable Poisson probability model.

(c) Conduct a χ^2 goodness of fit test to assess the suitability of the model chosen.

3 The following data refer to the numbers of water fleas present in 50 samples of pond water.

Number of water fleas	2	3	4	5	6	7	8	9	10	11	12	13	14	15	16
Number of samples		1	1	2	2	2	6	7	4	5	7	3	5	3	1	1

(a) Find the mean and variance of the data.

(b) Fit a Poisson distribution to the data and test using the chi-squared distribution.

4 Over a number of months in the Second World War, 576 squares of territory with $\frac{1}{2}$ km sides were observed, and many flying bomb hits were recorded. The table gives the number of squares in which r hits were recorded.

r	0	1	2	3	4	5
Frequency	229	211	93	35	7	1

Calculate the frequencies which would be expected from a Poisson model having the same mean as these data, and compare these with the observed frequencies.

Conduct a χ^2 goodness of fit test on the data.

5 A statistician, Ladislaus von Bortkiewicz, published a pamphlet in 1898 which provided one of the most famous examples of data which seem to have a Poisson distribution. The number of men killed by horse kicks each year was recorded for each of the fourteen corps in the Prussian army from 1875 to 1894. The data are summarised below.

Men killed (X)	0	1	2	3	4	5+	Total
Observed frequency	144	91	32	11	2	0	280

(a) Using the sample mean as an estimate of λ, calculate the expected frequencies on the basis of a Poisson model having this mean.

(b) Compare the observed and expected frequencies and comment on whether you think the Poisson distribution you have used is a good fit for the data.

(c) Conduct a χ^2 goodness of fit test on the model and comment on your findings.

D The Normal distribution as an approximation to the Poisson distribution (answers p. 93)

When the mean, λ, is large (say 10), the Poisson distribution becomes symmetrical.

The graphs below show the probabilities that a Poisson distribution takes particular values of x for two different values of λ.

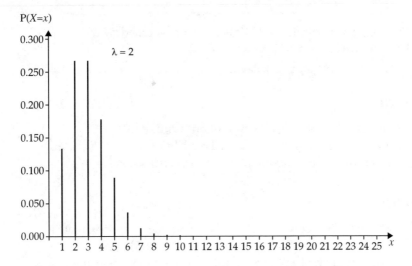

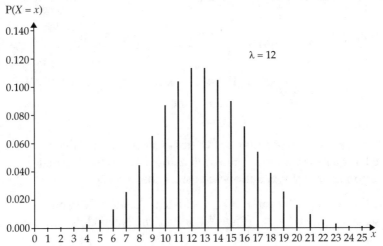

For $\lambda = 12$, the Poisson distribution has the familiar shape of the Normal distribution with one important difference.

The Normal distribution is a continuous one. It describes a variable which can take any value within a given range. The Poisson distribution is discrete. If we wish to compare a Normal distribution with a Poisson distribution, we need to choose an appropriate Normal distribution, and then think about how we can use it to describe a variable which can only take discrete values.

A Normal distribution can be described fully if we know its mean and variance. If we are choosing a Normal distribution to approximate a Poisson distribution, they must have the same mean and variance.

We therefore approximate the Poisson distribution $P(\lambda)$ with the Normal distribution $N(\lambda, \lambda)$. We can then use the tables for the standard Normal distribution to give us the probabilities that X will take values in a particular range.

> The Poisson distribution $P(\lambda)$ can be approximated by the Normal distribution $N(\lambda, \lambda)$ when $\lambda \geqslant 20$.

Example 2

For a random variable with Poisson distribution $P(20)$, $P(X = 14) = 0.0387$. Using the Normal distribution $N(20, 20)$ as an approximation to the Poisson distribution, calculate $P(X = 14)$.

Solution

Since we are using a continuous random variable to approximate a discrete variable, we will calculate $P(13.5 < X \leqslant 14.5)$. This is known as the **continuity correction**. First, standardise the variable using $\mu = \lambda = 20$ and $\sigma = \sqrt{\lambda} = \sqrt{20}$.

$$P(13.5 < X \leqslant 14.5) = P\left(\frac{13.5 - 20}{\sqrt{20}} < z \leqslant \frac{14.5 - 20}{\sqrt{20}}\right)$$
$$= \Phi(1.45) - \Phi(1.23)$$
$$= 0.9265 - 0.8907$$
$$= 0.0358$$

Where the probability of a range of values of a Poisson variable is required, rather than a single value, calculations using the Normal distribution as an approximation will usually be quicker.

1 For the Poisson distribution $P(30)$, calculate $P(25 \leqslant X \leqslant 30)$ and compare your answer with $P(25 \leqslant X \leqslant 30)$ for the Normal distribution $N(30, 30)$.

Exercise D (answers p. 93)

1 If $X \sim \text{P}(50)$ use the Normal approximation to find $\text{P}(X \leqslant 45)$.

2 A computer engineer knows that he replaces 20 computer fans in an average month. How many fans should he have in stock at the beginning of each month, if he wants to be 75% confident that he will not run out before the month end?

After working through this chapter you should

1 be able to choose a suitable probability model for counting cases data

2 be able to set up and test a chosen model

3 know how to calculate the number of degrees of freedom when modelling with the binomial, geometric and Poisson distributions

4 be able to make simple inferences on the basis of a chosen model

5 be able to use the standard Normal distribution to approximate the Poisson distribution when $\lambda \geqslant 20$.

5 Forming new variables

A Combining random variables (answers p. 94)

So far, the situations you have studied have each involved a single variable together with its associated probability distribution. There are many interesting situations where random variables are combined in some way. The chapter begins by considering **discrete random variables** and later extends the results to **continuous variables**.

These ideas were introduced in Chapter 7 of *Statistics 1* but will be considered in more detail here.

As an illustration, consider a game which has two options.

Option 1: Two dice are thrown and you win 1p for each point. Your score is the *total* score showing on the two dice.

Option 2: A single dice is thrown and you win 1p per point, your score being double that shown on the dice.

The entry price is the same for both games. Which would you choose to play and why?

It is clear that the mean winnings on the two games will be the same. However, the probability distributions for the two games are very different.

For option 1, the score X can take values from 2 to 12. The probabilities of the extreme scores are

$$P(X = 2) = \tfrac{1}{6} \times \tfrac{1}{6} = \tfrac{1}{36}$$
$$P(X = 12) = \tfrac{1}{36}$$

You could work out the probabilities for each value of X and the distribution would be:

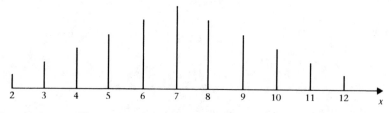

For option 2, all scores are equally likely. The only possible values of X are 2, 4, 6, 8, 10 and 12 and the distribution is as follows.

You *cannot* alter your expected winnings by your choice of game. Option 2 offers you a greater chance of winning a large amount but, at the same time, a greater chance of winning only a small amount.

The methods developed in this section will enable you to analyse this problem in greater detail, and you will have a chance to come back to it later on.

Many situations involve combining random variables. For example, the total weight of passengers on an aircraft is a random variable (with its own mean and variance) made up of a sum of independent random variables, each having its own mean and variance. How is the mean related to the means of the individual variables? How are the variances related? You can start to consider this important problem below, and develop some useful results for your later work.

The probability distributions for two packs of cards are shown below. Y is the score on a card from the yellow pack.

y	1	2	3	4	Mean	$= 2$
$P(Y=y)$	0.4	0.3	0.2	0.1	Variance	$= 1$

For the blue pack, the distribution of the score, B, is

b	1	2	4	Mean	$= 2$
$P(B=b)$	0.25	0.50	0.25	Variance	$= 0.5$

A game consists of selecting a card at random from the yellow pack and noting its score (Y). A second card is then selected from the blue pack (B) and the total score ($Y + B$) recorded.
All possible totals ($Y + B$) are shown in the table.

		Score on blue card		
		1	2	3
Score on	1	2	3	4
yellow card	2	3	4	5
	3	4	5	6
	4	5	6	7

The probability of obtaining a score of 3 is
$$P(3) = P(1, 2) + P(2, 1)$$
$$= 0.4 \times 0.5 + 0.3 \times 0.25$$
$$= 0.275$$

1 (a) Show that $P(5) = 0.20$ and complete the probability distribution for the total score $Y + B$.

(b) Find the mean and variance of $Y + B$. How are the mean and variance of $Y + B$ related to those of Y and B?

Score $Y + B$	Probability
2	
3	0.275
4	
5	0.20
6	0.10
7	

2 Write down the probability distributions for the new variables $2B$ and $3Y$. In each case, calculate the mean and variance and show how they are related to the means and variances of B and Y respectively.

You have considered combining random variables in two ways:

- adding two (or more) together, for example, $Y + B$
- multiplying by a constant, for example, $2Y$, $5B$, and so on.

The above examples should lead you to *conjecture* the following results:

$$\text{Mean } (X + Y) = \text{mean } (X) + \text{mean } (Y)$$
$$\text{Variance } (X + Y) = \text{variance } (X) + \text{variance } (Y)$$
$$\text{Mean } (aX) = a \times \text{mean } (X)$$
$$\text{Variance } (aX) = a^2 \times \text{variance } (X)$$

You should note that the variables you have combined have been *independent* and *discrete*. The results obtained above can be proved for *all* independent random variables.

Example 1

In a game using two spinners, the score is counted as the total of the score on each spinner. The probability distributions for the two spinners are given in the tables.

Spinner 1			
Score	1	2	3
Probability	$\frac{1}{2}$	$\frac{1}{4}$	$\frac{1}{4}$

Spinner 2		
Score	2	4
Probability	$\frac{1}{4}$	$\frac{3}{4}$

It costs 20p to have a go and you win five times the total score on the two spinners in pence.

(a) Calculate the probability of a score of five.

(b) What is the most likely score?

(c) Calculate your expected winnings per turn.

Solution

(a) $P(\text{total} = 5) = P(1, 4) + P(3, 2)$

$$= \tfrac{1}{2} \times \tfrac{3}{4} + \tfrac{1}{4} \times \tfrac{1}{4} \quad \text{(the events are independent)}$$

$$= \tfrac{7}{16}$$

(b) The most likely score is five.

$$P(\text{total} = 3) = \tfrac{1}{8}, \ P(\text{total} = 4) = \tfrac{1}{16}, \ P(\text{total} = 6) = \tfrac{3}{16},$$

$$P(\text{total} = 7) = \tfrac{3}{16}$$

(c) Let S_1 and S_2 be the scores on the two spinners.

Expected net winnings $= (5 \times \text{mean score}) - 20$

Expected score $= \text{mean } (S_1 + S_2)$

$\qquad\qquad\qquad\quad = \text{mean}(S_1) + \text{mean}(S_2)$

$\text{Mean}(S_1) = \tfrac{7}{4}, \text{mean}(S_2) = \tfrac{14}{4}$

$\Rightarrow \quad \text{Mean } (S_1 + S_2) = \tfrac{7}{4} + \tfrac{14}{4} = \tfrac{21}{4}$

The mean net winnings are $\dfrac{5 \times 21}{4} - 20 = 6.25\text{p}$

You would expect to win an average of 6.25 pence per game.

3 Use these ideas and results to analyse the dice games described at the start of the chapter.

New random variables may also be formed by subtraction. If A and B are random variables, then $A - B$ is also a random variable.

4 (a) List the probability distribution for $A - B$ where A and B have probability distributions as follows.

a	0	1	2	b	1	2
$P(a)$	0.2	0.6	0.2	$P(b)$	0.5	0.5

(b) Confirm these.

(i) $\text{Mean}(A - B) = \text{mean}(A) - \text{mean}(B)$

(ii) $\text{Variance}(A - B) = \text{variance}(A) + \text{variance}(B)$

The earlier results on combining random variables can be simply extended.

For independent random variables X and Y,

$$\text{Mean } (X \pm Y) = \text{mean}(X) \pm \text{mean}(Y)$$
$$\text{Variance } (X \pm Y) = \text{variance}(X) + \text{variance}(Y)$$

Example 2

Independent random variables
A, *B* and *C* have the following
means and variances.

	A	B	C
Mean	4	2	3
Variance	2	1	2

Write down the mean and variance of these.

(a) $2A - B$ (b) $A + B - C$ (c) $2A + 2B - 3C$

Solution

(a) $\text{Mean}(2A - B) = 2\,\text{mean}(A) - \text{mean}(B)$
$$= 6$$
$\text{Variance}(2A - B) = 2^2\,\text{variance}(A) + \text{variance}(B)$
$$= 9$$

(b) $\text{Mean}(A + B - C) = 4 + 2 - 3 = 3$
$\text{Variance}(A + B - C) = 2 + 1 + 2 = 5$

(c) $\text{Mean}(2A + 2B - 3C) = 2 \times 4 + 2 \times 2 - 3 \times 3 = 3$
$\text{Variance}(2A + 2B - 3C) = 2^2 \times 2 + 2^2 \times 1 + 3^2 \times 2 = 30$

Exercise A (answers p. 95)

1 A board game uses a cuboid roller with square cross-section to
determine how many places forward a player moves. The four
rectangular faces are numbered 1, 2, 5 and 8 .

(a) If *X* is the score obtained by rolling the cuboid, find these.

(i) mean(*X*)   (ii) variance(*X*)

(b) If, during the game, a player lands on a yellow square, the next
score on the roller is doubled. Find the mean and variance of the
doubled scores.

(c) If, during the game, a player lands on a red square, the next score
on the roller is trebled. Find the mean and variance of the trebled
scores.

(d) Write down the mean and variance of the total score obtained
when two identical rollers are used together.

2 (a) A cubical dice has its faces numbered 1, 2, 2, 3, 3 and 4 . If *X* is the
score obtained by rolling the dice, find the mean and variance of
the scores.

(b) A second dice has its faces numbered 2, 4, 4, 6, 6 and 8 . What are
the mean and variance of the scores?

(c) Write down the mean and variance of the total score when both
dice are rolled.

3   If X and Y are independent random single-digit numbers from 1 to 9 inclusive, calculate the variance of these.

(a) X (b) $2X$ (c) $X+Y$ (d) $2X-Y$

4   Each of the variables X_1, X_2, X_3 independently takes values from the set $\{-1, 0, 1\}$ with probabilities 0.2, 0.6, 0.2 respectively; the variable Y is defined to be the median of X_1, X_2, X_3.

(a) Show that $P(Y=-1) = 0.104$ and deduce $P(Y=1)$ and $P(Y=0)$.

(b) Calculate the mean and variance of Y.

B Combining Poisson variables (answers p. 95)

For Poisson variables, the following result can be proved, although we do not do so here. (γ is the Greek letter g, 'gamma'.)

> If X and Y are independently distributed Poisson variables having means λ and γ respectively, then $X+Y$ is also a Poisson variable.
>
> $X+Y \sim P(\lambda + \gamma)$

Example 3

Cars stopping at a roadside garage come from either the north-bound or south-bound traffic. On average, there are three cars from the south-bound lane in a 15-minute interval and 1.6 cars from the north-bound lane every 15 minutes. The number of arrivals has a Poisson distribution in both cases.

Calculate these probabilities.

(a) No cars arrive from the north-bound lane in a 15-minute interval.

(b) More than two cars arrive in a 15-minute interval.

Solution

(a) Let the number of cars stopping from the north-bound lane be N.

$N \sim P(1.6)$ $P(N=0) = e^{-1.6} = 0.202$

(b) The total number of cars stopping is $T = N + S$

$T \sim P(3 + 1.6)$ or $T \sim P(4.6)$

$P(T > 2) = 1 - P(T = 0, 1, 2)$

$$= 1 - \left(e^{-4.6} + 4.6e^{-4.6} + \frac{4.6^2 e^{-4.6}}{2!} \right)$$

$$= 1 - e^{-4.6}\left(1 + 4.6 + \frac{4.6^2}{2} \right) = 0.837$$

In Chapter 4 you noted, but did not prove, that the variance of a Poisson distribution is equal to its mean. The variable T in the example above will have mean and variance $= 3 + 1.6 = 4.6$.

Exercise B (answers p. 95)

1 X and Y have independent Poisson distributions, where

$$X \sim P(4) \qquad \text{and} \qquad Y \sim P(3)$$

(a) Write down the mean of $X + Y$.

(b) Calculate the probability that $X + Y < 4$.

2   An executive has two telephones on her desk which receive calls independently. The number of calls received by each telephone has a Poisson distribution with, on average, 3 calls per five-minute interval on one and 2 calls per five-minute interval on the other.

(a) Write down the mean and variance of the *total* number of calls received in a five-minute interval.

(b) Find the probability that these numbers of calls are received in any five-minute interval.

(i) 0   (ii) More than 2

3   Cars arrive at a garage for petrol from either the north-bound or the south bound carriageway. There are on average 3 cars every five minutes travelling north and 1.8 cars every five minutes travelling south.

(a) Calculate the probability that these numbers of cars arrive at the garage in a particular five-minute interval.

(i) No cars   (ii) More than 2

(b) Calculate the probability that exactly 5 cars arrive in a ten-minute interval.

C Expectation and variance (answers p. 95)

This section uses notation introduced in Chapter 7 of *Statistics 1*.

> The expected value, or expectation, of a random variable (X) is the mean value of the variable. It is written $E[X]$.

For a discrete random variable,

$$\text{Mean}(X) = \sum_i x_i P(x_i) = E[X]$$

$$\text{Mean}(2X) = \sum_i 2x_i P(x_i) = E[2X]$$

$$\text{Mean}(X^2) = \sum_i x_i^2 P(x_i) = E[X^2]$$

So the result $\text{Mean}(X + Y) = \text{mean}(X) + \text{mean}(Y)$
obtained in Section A can be written

$$E[X + Y] = E[X] + E[Y]$$

Example 4

The probability distribution of X is given in the table.

x	1	2
$P(X = x)$	0.2	0.8

(a) Find the expected value of X^3.
(b) Find the expected value of $2X^2$.

Solution

(a) X^3 can take the values 1^3 and 2^3 with probabilities 0.2 and 0.8
     respectively.
     $E[X^3] = 1^3 \times 0.2 + 2^3 \times 0.8$
     $= 6.6$

(b) $E[2X^2] = 2 \times 1^2 \times 0.2 + 2 \times 2^2 \times 0.8$
     $= 6.8$

A convenient shorthand for the variance is $V[X]$. The variance may be
defined in terms of expectations as follows.

$$V[X] = \sum_i x_i^2 P(x_i) - \mu^2$$

But $\sum_i x_i^2 P(x_i) = E[X^2]$ and $\mu = E[X]$.

So,

$$V[X] = E[X^2] - (E[X])^2$$

1 If X takes the values $x_1, x_2, \ldots, x_n$, prove these.

(a) $E[aX] = aE[X]$

(b) $E[X + b] = E[X] + b$

(c) $V[aX] = a^2 V[X]$

The results of Section A may be written as follows.

$$E[X \pm Y] = E[X] \pm E[Y]$$
$$V[X \pm Y] = V[X] + V[Y]$$
$$E[aX] = a \times E[X]$$
$$V[aX] = a^2 \times V[X]$$

Example 5

Two random variables X and Y are such that $E[X] = V[X] = 1$, $E[Y] = 3$ and $V[Y] = 2$. Find these.

(a) $E[X - Y]$ (b) $V[3X - 2Y]$

Solution

(a) $E[X - Y] = E[X] - E[Y] = -2$

(b) $V[3X - 2Y] = V[3X] + V[2Y]$
$$= 3^2 V[X] + 2^2 V[Y]$$
$$= 17$$

General proofs for the results

$$E[X + Y] = E[X] + E[Y]$$

and

$$V[X + Y] = V[X] + V[Y]$$

are difficult because of the complexity of the notation. However, the questions below illustrate how the proof would proceed.

Consider two discrete random variables X and Y. Suppose X can take only the values x_1, x_2 and x_3 and Y only y_1 and y_2. The probability distributions of X and Y are given in these tables.

x	x_1	x_2	x_3	y	y_1	y_2
$P(X = x)$	a	b	c	$P(Y = y)$	d	e

There are only six possible values of the variable $X + Y$, having probabilities r, s, t, u, v, w, for example.

2E List the six possible values of $X + Y$.

The probabilities associated with each of the possible values are shown in the table below.

		X values		
		x_1	x_2	x_3
Y values	y_1	r	s	t	d
	y_2	u	v	w	e
		a	b	c	1

$P(x_3 + y_2) = w$

$u + v + w = e$

$s + v = b$

If X and Y were independent, we could calculate, for example, that $r = ad$, but it is not necessary for this proof that the random variables should be independent.

3E Explain why these are true.

(a) $r + u = a$ (b) $r + s + t = d$ (c) $d + e = 1$

Using the probabilities defined in the table,

$$E[X + Y] = (x_1 + y_1)r + (x_2 + y_1)s + (x_3 + y_1)t$$
$$+ (x_1 + y_2)u + (x_2 + y_2)v + (x_3 + y_2)w$$
$$= x_1(r + u) + x_2(s + v) + x_3(t + w)$$
$$+ y_1(r + s + t) + y_2(u + v + w)$$
$$= x_1 a + x_2 b + x_3 c + y_1 d + y_2 e$$
$$= E[X] + E[Y]$$

To obtain the variance relationship, use the result

$$V[X] = E[X^2] - (E[X])^2$$

So,

$$V[X + Y] = E[(X + Y)^2] - (E[X + Y])^2$$
$$= E[X^2] + E[Y^2] + 2E[XY] - (E[X] + E[Y])^2$$
$$= E[X^2] - (E[X])^2 + E[Y^2] - (E[Y])^2$$
$$+ 2E[XY] - 2E[X]E[Y] \qquad (1)$$

4E If X and Y are *independent* random variables, $P(xy) = P(x)P(y)$. Using this result, and the relationships between the various probabilities shown in the table, prove that $E[XY] = E[X]E[Y]$.

For independent random variables X and Y, $E[XY] = E[X]E[Y]$ and so expression (1) simplifies to

$$V[X + Y] = E[X^2] - (E[X])^2 + E[Y^2] - (E[Y])^2$$
$$= V[X] + V[Y]$$

(X and Y *must* be independent variables).

A more general proof extends to n values for X $(x_1, x_2, \ldots, x_i, \ldots, x_n)$ and m values for Y $(y_1, y_2, \ldots, y_j, \ldots, y_m)$.

Results for continuous random variables

Just as for a discrete random variable, the following results for a continuous random variable can be obtained using integration in place of summation.

$$E[X] = \int x f(x) dx$$

$$E[2X] = \int 2x f(x) dx = 2 \int x f(x) dx = 2E[X]$$

$$E[X + 3] = \int (x + 3) f(x) dx = \int x f(x) dx + \int 3 f(x) dx$$
$$= E[X] + 3 \int f(x) dx = E[X] + 3$$

$$E[X^2] = \int x^2 f(x) dx$$

$$E[X^{-1}] = \int \frac{1}{x} f(x) dx$$

and if X and Y are independent continuous random variables, then

$$E[X + Y] = E[X] + E[Y]$$

5 Continuous random variables X and Y have these probability density functions.

$$f(x) = \begin{cases} 0 & \text{for} & x < 0 \\ 1 & \text{for} & 0 \leqslant x < 1 \\ 0 & \text{for} & 1 \leqslant x \end{cases} \qquad g(y) = \begin{cases} 0 & \text{for} & y < 0 \\ 2 & \text{for} & 0 \leqslant y < 0.5 \\ 0 & \text{for} & 0.5 \leqslant y \end{cases}$$

Calculate $E[X]$, $E[Y]$ and $E[X + Y]$.

Similarly we can extend our results for variances of discrete random variables to continuous random variables.

By definition

$$V[X] = \int (x - \mu)^2 f(x) dx \quad \text{where } \mu = E[X]$$

$$= \int (x^2 - 2\mu x + \mu^2) f(x) dx$$

$$= \int x^2\, f(x)dx - \int 2\mu x\, f(x)dx + \int \mu^2\, f(x)dx$$

$$= E[X^2] - 2\mu \int x\, f(x)dx + \int \mu^2\, f(x)dx$$

$$= E[X^2] - 2\mu E[X] + \mu^2 \int f(x)dx$$

$$= E[X^2] - 2\mu^2 + \mu^2$$

$$= E[X^2] - \mu^2$$

For some multiple a,

$$V[aX] = E[(aX)^2] - (a\mu)^2$$
$$= a^2 E[X^2] - a^2 \mu^2$$
$$= a^2 V[X]$$

It is also true, although not proved here, that for independent continuous random variables X and Y,

$$V[X + Y] = V[X - Y] = V[X] + V[Y]$$

6 A continuous random variable T has probability density function

$$f(t) = \begin{cases} 0 & \text{for} \quad t < 1 \\[2mm] \dfrac{5}{4t^2} & \text{for} \quad 1 \leqslant t \leqslant 5 \end{cases}$$

Calculate $E[T]$ and $V[T]$.

7 Independent continuous random variables X and Y have probability density functions

$$f(x) = \begin{cases} 0 & \text{for} & x < 0 \\ \frac{1}{2}x & \text{for} & 0 \leqslant x < 2 \\ 0 & \text{for} & x \geqslant 2 \end{cases}$$

$$g(y) = \begin{cases} 0 & \text{for} & y < 0 \\ 2 & \text{for} & 0 \leqslant y < \frac{1}{2} \\ 0 & \text{for} & \frac{1}{2} \leqslant y \end{cases}$$

Calculate $E[X + Y]$ and $V[X + Y]$.

D Some proofs (answers p. 96)

Of the three discrete distributions considered in Chapter 2 – geometric, binomial and Poisson – a proof of the results for the mean and variance has, so far, only been given for the binomial (see *Statistics 1*, Chapter 7). In this section you will consider the other two discrete distributions and prove similar results for a continuous distribution, the exponential distribution.

The geometric distribution

If $X \sim G(p)$, then $E[X]$ is the number of trials needed until the required event occurs.

1D How long do you think you would wait, on average, until you score a six when you throw a dice?

If $X \sim G(p)$, then $E[X] = \sum_i iP(X=i)$

Writing this out in full gives
$$E[X] = 1p + 2pq + 3pq^2 + \dots$$
$$= p(1 + 2q + 3q^2 + \dots)$$

2 Confirm that the expression in brackets is the binomial expansion of $(1-q)^{-2}$.

$$E[X] = \frac{p}{(1-q)^2} = \frac{1}{p}$$

For throwing a six with a dice, $X \sim G(\frac{1}{6})$. You would expect to wait six throws on average because $E[X] = 6$.

The Poisson distribution

Suppose X is a Poisson variable, $X \sim P(\lambda)$.

$$E[X] = \sum_i iP(X=i) \qquad \text{where } P(X=r) = \frac{e^{-\lambda}\lambda^r}{r!}$$

In the proofs which follow you will need the series expansion for e^x.

$$e^x = 1 + x + \frac{x^2}{2!} + \frac{x^3}{3!} + \dots + \frac{x^n}{n!} + \dots$$

3E Complete the following proof.

$$E[X] = \frac{0 \times e^{-\lambda}\lambda^0}{0!} + \frac{1 \times e^{-\lambda}\lambda}{1!} + \dots$$
$$= e^{-\lambda}\{(\dots) + (\dots) + (\dots) + \dots\}$$
$$= \lambda e^{-\lambda}\{\dots + \dots + \dots + \dots\}$$
$$= \lambda e^{-\lambda}e^{\lambda} \quad \text{using the expansion of } e^x$$
$$= \lambda$$

To obtain the variance, you will need to use
$$V[X] = E[X^2] - (E[X])^2 \quad \text{where } E[X] = \lambda$$
Finding $E[X^2]$ is awkward here. It is best to use an algebraic 'trick' and to work with $E[X(X-1)]$.

4E Show that
$$E[X^2] = E[X(X-1)] + E[X]$$

To use this result, you need to find an expression for $E[X(X-1)]$.

$$E[X(X-1)] = \sum_i x_i(x_i-1)P(x_i)$$

$$= \frac{2 \times 1 \times e^{-\lambda}\lambda^2}{2!} + \frac{3 \times 2 \times e^{-\lambda}\lambda^3}{3!} + \dots$$

5E Complete the proof to show these.

(a) $E[X(X-1)] = \lambda^2$

(b) $V[X] = \lambda$

This confirms a useful result you have already met for Poisson variables – that the mean and the variance are equal. When considering whether data appear to conform to the Poisson model, this is a rough test you can apply.

> If X is a random variable with a Poisson probability distribution,
>
> Mean (X) = variance(X)

The exponential distribution

6E X is a random variable with probability density function $f(x)$, where

$$f(x) = \lambda e^{-\lambda x} \quad \text{for } x \geqslant 0$$

X is said to have an exponential distribution.

An example of an exponential distribution is the length of waiting times between random events.

(a) Prove that $E[X] = \dfrac{1}{\lambda}$.

(b) Prove that $V[X] = \dfrac{1}{\lambda^2}$.

E Combining Normal random variables (answers p. 97)

Some important practical applications of the results of this chapter arise where Normal variables are combined. Remember that the variables being combined must be *independent* of each other.

A common example is as follows. All passenger lifts have a notice specifying the maximum load and usually state the maximum number of persons that can be carried safely. The maximum number of persons is determined from the maximum load by considering the distribution of the total weight of n adult males. The weight of an adult male is well modelled by a Normal variable, so the manufacturer needs to consider the problem of adding together Normal variables.

When you add independently distributed Normal variables, you need to know the answers to three questions.

(a) How is the sum *distributed?* Is it also a Normal variable?

(b) What is its mean value and how is this related to the original parameters?

(c) What is its variance and how is this related to the original parameters?

Questions (b) and (c) were answered in Sections A and C. The results you found there also apply to *continuous* variables.

Although the result is beyond the scope of this book to prove theoretically, it can be shown that the sum or difference of *independent* Normal variables is also Normally distributed: if X and Y are independent Normal random variables, then

$$\left.\begin{array}{l} Z = X + Y \\ M = X - Y \\ P = X + X + Y \\ \text{and so on} \dots \end{array}\right\} \text{are also Normal random variables.}$$

These results may be summarised as follows.

A sum or difference of *independent* Normal random variables is also Normally distributed.

If X and Y are independent random variables, where

$$X \sim N(\mu_x, \sigma_x^2) \qquad \text{and} \qquad Y \sim N(\mu_y, \sigma_y^2)$$

then

$$X + Y \sim N(\mu_x + \mu_y, \sigma_x^2 + \sigma_y^2)$$

and

$$X - Y \sim N(\mu_x - \mu_y, \sigma_x^2 + \sigma_y^2)$$

These results can be used to solve problems like that of the maximum load for a lift. Some simple examples are given.

Example 6

If $X \sim N(10, 2)$ and $Y \sim N(8, 1)$, find $P(X + Y > 20)$.

Solution

Variances are added

$X + Y \sim N(10 + 8, 2 + 1)$
$X + Y \sim N(18, 3)$

Standardising the value $X + Y = 20$

$$\Rightarrow \quad z = \frac{20 - 18}{\sqrt{3}}$$
$$= 1.15$$
$$\Rightarrow \quad P(X + Y > 20) = 1 - \Phi(1.15)$$
$$= 1 - 0.875$$
$$= 0.125$$

So, in $12\frac{1}{2}\%$ of cases the value of the sum of the two variables will be greater than 20.

Example 7

The length (in centimetres) of a matchbox is a random variable $X \sim N(5, 0.01)$.
The length (in centimetres) of matches to go in the box is a random variable, $Y \sim N(4.6, 0.01)$.

What percentage of matches will not fit in the box?

Solution

The matches will not fit if $Y > X$. This condition can be rearranged as $X - Y < 0$.

$$E[X - Y] = 5 - 4.6$$
$$= 0.4$$
$$V[X - Y] = 0.01 + 0.01$$
$$= 0.02$$
$$\Rightarrow X - Y \sim N(0.4, 0.02)$$

Add variances

You need to find the shaded area. Standardising in the usual way,

$$z = \frac{0.0 - 0.4}{\sqrt{0.02}}$$

$$= -2.83$$

$$P(Z < 0) = \Phi(-2.83)$$

$$= 1 - \Phi(2.83)$$

$$= 0.0023$$

So only about 0.2% of matches will not fit into a randomly selected box.

Exercise E (answers p. 97)

1   A manufacturer of toiletries is producing a special offer pack containing a deodorant spray and a bar of soap. The deodorant spray can has a length (in centimetres) given by the random variable $X \sim N(14, 0.02)$. The soap has a length (in centimetres) given by the random variable $Y \sim N(9, 0.01)$.

   Find the probability that the deodorant and soap will not fit a container of length 23.4 cm if they are packed end to end.

2   A bottle of shampoo has a stopper which has length (in centimetres) given by the random variable $X \sim N(3, 0.003)$. The length of the bottle in centimetres, not including the stopper, is given by the random variable $Y \sim N(20, 0.06)$.

   What percentage of bottles will not fit on a shelf with a space of 23.5 cm below the next shelf?

3   The thickness in centimetres of an Oatbix is given by a random variable $X \sim N(1.9, 0.01)$. There are twelve Oatbix in a packet. What percentage of boxes that are 24 cm long are too small?

4   A storage cupboard has width X cm, where $X \sim N(79, 1.25)$. What is the probability that five similar cupboards placed side by side will fit along a wall 3.98 m long?

5   The internal diameter (in millimetres) of a nut is a random variable $X \sim N(10, 0.013)$. The diameter (in millimetres) of a bolt is a random variable $Y \sim N(9.5, 0.013)$.

   (a) If the difference between the two diameters is less than 0.2 mm, the nut and bolt jam tight. What percentage of nuts and bolts jam?

   (b) If the difference between the two diameters is more than 0.75 mm, the nut and bolt are too loose. What percentage of nuts and bolts are too loose?

6 A small saucepan lid has an external diameter (in centimetres) given by the random variable $X \sim N(18, 0.005)$. The saucepan has an internal diameter (in centimetres) given by the random variable $Y \sim N(18.2, 0.005)$.

What percentage of the lids do not fit their saucepans if the gap must never be less than 0.05 cm?

After working through this chapter you should

1 know that random variables may be combined to give composite variables.

2 understand the term **expectation** as applied to random variables and be familiar with the notation of expectation

3 know that for *independent* random variables:

    (a) $E[X \pm Y] = E[X] \pm E[Y]$
    (b) $V[X \pm Y] = V[X] + V[Y]$

4 know that for a Poisson variable $E[X] = V[X] = \lambda$

5 know how to combine two independent Poisson variables and know and be able to use the result
if

$$X \sim P(\lambda) \qquad \text{and} \qquad Y \sim P(\gamma)$$

then

$$X + Y \sim P(\lambda + \gamma)$$

6 know how to combine two or more independent Normal variables and know and be able to use the result
if

$$X \sim N(\mu_x, \sigma_x^2), \quad Y \sim N(\mu_y, \sigma_y^2)$$

then

$$X \pm Y \sim N(\mu_x \pm \mu_y, \sigma_x^2 + \sigma_y^2)$$

6 Hypothesis testing

A Making a decision: the null hypothesis (answers p. 98)

The following results were established earlier in the course and will be needed to analyse this problem. (See *Statistics 1*, Chapter 7, and Chapter 4 of this book.)

- For $R \sim B(n, p)$

$$P(R = r) = \binom{n}{r} p^r (1 - p)^{n-r} \text{ where } \binom{n}{r} = \frac{n!}{r!(n-r)!}$$

mean $= np$ and variance $= np(1 - p)$

- The Normal approximation to the binomial is often used to estimate probabilities such as $P(R \geqslant 14)$.

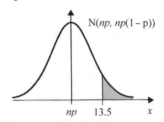

A teacher has a set of loaded dice which are biased in such a way that the probability of any one of these dice showing a six is $\frac{1}{4}$. The loaded dice have become mixed up with a set of ordinary dice so she hands out all the dice to her students and asks them to throw each dice sixty times. If a dice shows a six on fourteen or more occasions she decides it must be 'loaded'. Otherwise it is classified as 'fair'. The students are then asked to discuss this method of sorting the dice.

1D

(a) What is the probability that a dice is classified as 'loaded' when in fact it is 'fair'?

(b) What is the probability that a dice is classified as 'fair' when in fact it is 'loaded'?

(c) Do you think the teacher should change her threshold for rejecting a dice as 'fair' from fourteen to each of these values?

(i) Thirteen (ii) Fifteen (iii) Some other value

Justify your answer.

(d) Suppose a dice showed a six on just two occasions. How would you interpret such a result?

In the example above, if you start with the assumption that a dice is 'fair', then this is called the **null hypothesis**. The **alternative hypothesis** is that the dice is 'loaded'.

The conventional shorthand for expressing these hypotheses is:

$H_0: p = \frac{1}{6}$ (The null hypothesis)

$H_1: p = \frac{1}{4}$ (The alternative hypothesis)

In this case, you could put a specific value on the alternative hypothesis. This is not always possible.

Suppose a student arranges a number of glasses on a table to test whether a friend can tell the difference between 'diet' cola and 'ordinary' cola. (Each glass is filled at random with either 'diet' or 'ordinary' cola.) He asks his friend, who claims to be able to taste the difference, to taste each in turn and identify what is in each glass.

2D

State whether you think the null and alternative hypotheses for this experiment should be

$H_0: p = \frac{1}{2}$

$H_1: p > \frac{1}{2}$

or

$H_0: p = \frac{1}{2}$

$H_1: p \neq \frac{1}{2}$

where p is the probability that the friend makes a correct identification. Justify your answer.

A hypothesis is an assumption about the population from which the data have been sampled.

The null hypothesis (H_0) is the assumption against which the data are initially compared.

If, after comparison, the null hypothesis appears unlikely, it is rejected in favour of the alternative hypothesis (H_1).

B Making the wrong decision (answers p. 99)

A farmer knows from experience that the yield he obtains from a particular type of tomato plant is Normally distributed with a mean of 6.2 kg and standard deviation 1.8 kg. A friend claims to be able to increase the yield of a plant by talking to it. They decide to put this claim to the test. A plant is selected at random and the farmer's friend talks to it for at least half an hour a day during its growing season.

If μ is the yield in kilograms of a tomato plant which has received the treatment, then the null and alternative hypotheses are:

$H_0: \mu = 6.2$

$H_1: \mu > 6.2$

The farmer says that he will be convinced if the plant's yield, X, exceeds 10 kg. His friend disagrees and feels that the farmer should accept the alternative hypothesis if the plant yields more than 9 kg.

Rejecting H_0 when in fact it is the correct hypothesis is called a **type I error**.

Accepting H_0 when in fact H_1 is the correct hypothesis is called a **type II error**.

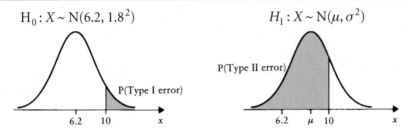

$H_0 : X \sim N(6.2, 1.8^2)$ $H_1 : X \sim N(\mu, \sigma^2)$

P(Type II error)

P(Type I error)

Notice that the alternative hypothesis does not make any assumptions about the variance of the yield.

1 Calculate the probability of a type I error if H_0 is rejected for $X > 10$.

2 Explain why it is not possible to calculate the probability of a type II error.

3 What would be the probability of a type I error if H_0 is rejected for $X > 9$?

4 If it is decided to reject H_0 for $X > 9$ rather than $X > 10$, will the probability of a type II error increase or decrease?

5 The farmer and his friend agree that a probability of 5% for a type I error is reasonable. For what value of x is $P(X > x) = 0.05$?

C Level of significance (answers p. 99)

The cornerstone of English law is that a person is assumed innocent until proved guilty. Similarly, a null hypothesis is accepted until there is sufficient evidence to 'prove' it false.

A null hypothesis is rejected in favour of an alternative hypothesis when the observed data (the evidence) fall into a **critical region**. However, there is always a chance of rejecting a null hypothesis when in fact it is correct, just as there is always a chance of convicting an innocent person in a court of law. The probability of a type I error is the **significance level** of the test. Data which fall into the 5% critical region are said to be **significant at the 5% level**.

If the critical region is in just one tail of the distribution, then the test is called a one-tail test. If the critical region is split equally between the two tails, then the test is called a two-tail test. Whether a test is a one-tail test or a two-tail test depends on the alternative hypothesis.

One-tail test

H_0 : mean $= \mu$

H_1 : mean $> \mu$

The critical region at the 5% level is

$\qquad X > \mu + 1.645\sigma$

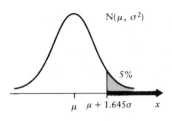

Two-tail test

H_0 : mean $= \mu$

H_1 : mean $\neq \mu$

The critical region at the 5% level is

$\qquad X < \mu - 1.96\sigma \quad$ or $\quad X > \mu + 1.96\sigma$

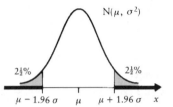

1 Draw similar diagrams to show the critical regions of a Normal distribution for one- and two-tail tests when the level of significance takes these values.

(a) 1%   (b) 0.1%

> In hypothesis testing, statisticians adopt the following convention to describe the significance of observed data.
>
> ● Data which occur in the critical region at the 5% level of significance are called *significant*.
>
> ● Data which occur in the critical region at the 1% level of significance are called *very significant*.
>
> ● Data which occur in the critical region at the 0.1% level of significance are called *highly significant*.

The choice of a significance level will depend on how important it is to avoid a type I error.

Example 1

Last year Lisbeth was elected president of the students' union when 40% of members supported her. She claims that her support has increased during her year in office. The college magazine selects 150 students at random for a survey and finds that 75 say they will vote for her this year. Does this provide significant evidence for an increase in her support?

Solution

Assuming that her support is unchanged, if the number of students who support her in a random sample of 150 is r, then $R \sim B(150, 0.4)$.

$H_0 : p = 0.4$

$H_1 : p > 0.4$

Level of significance: 5%

The Normal approximation to the binomial is $X \sim N(60, 36)$.

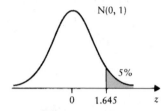

N(0, 1)

$$z = \frac{74.5 - 60}{\sqrt{36}} \approx 2.42$$

5%

0   1.645 z

As the result of the survey falls in the critical region, you should reject H_0 and conclude that there has been a significant increase in her support.

The following result was established in Chapter 6 of *Statistics 1*.

The Central Limit Theorem states that if $X \sim N(\mu, \sigma^2)$ then the distribution of sample means is $\overline{X} \sim N\left(\mu, \frac{\sigma^2}{n}\right)$.

Example 2

You can buy a cup of cola from a drinks machine. The amount dispensed, 300 ml, varies slightly. If X is the amount dispensed in millilitres, then $X \sim N(300, 10^2)$.

The operator samples four cups and accurately measures their contents. If the sample mean is significantly different from the expected value, she resets the machine.

Calculate the 'acceptable' range of values for the sample mean.

Solution

$H_0 : \mu = 300$

$H_1 : \mu \neq 300$

Level of significance: 5%

The distribution of sample means is Normally distributed:

$$\overline{X} \sim N\left(300, \frac{10^2}{4}\right)$$

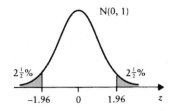

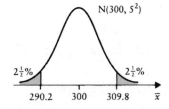

The region of acceptance is $300 - 1.96 \times 5 < \overline{X} < 300 + 1.96 \times 5$

or $\qquad 290.2 < \overline{X} < 309.8$

Example 3

Hourly failures of a component in a critical control system have a Poisson distribution with mean 1.2 . A new supplier is found for the components, and once they have all been replaced, failures in the system are monitored for one hour. Four components fail in this time and the system manager decides that the new components are less reliable. Test his conclusion at the 5% level.

Solution

The distribution of the number of component failures in one hour is $F \sim P(\lambda)$.

$H_0 : \lambda = 1.2$

$H_1 : \lambda > 1.2$

Level of significance: 5%

$$P(F \geqslant 4) =$$

$$= 1 - P(F = 0) - P(F = 1) - P(F = 2) - P(F = 3)$$

$$= 1 - e^{-1.2} - 1.2e^{-1.2} - \frac{1.2^2 e^{-1.2}}{2!} - \frac{1.2^3 e^{-1.2}}{3!}$$

$$= 0.034$$

There is evidence at the 5% level that λ has increased, and that the new components are less reliable.

Example 4

In a much larger control system, daily component failures are $F \sim P(120)$

After the components are replaced, 100 failures occur in the next 24 hours. The manager concludes that the new components are neither more nor less reliable. Test his conclusion at the 5% level.

Solution

$$F \sim P(\lambda)$$
$$H_0 : \lambda = 120$$
$$H_1 : \lambda \neq 120$$

Level of significance: 5%

Because $\lambda > 20$, we can use the Normal distribution as an approximation to the Poisson. Assume $F \sim N(120, \sqrt{120})$.

$$P(F < 100.5) = P\left(z < \frac{100.5 - 120}{\sqrt{120}}\right) = P(z < -1.780)$$

The critical region for a two-tail test at the 5% level is $z < -1.96$ or $z > +1.96$.

The evidence supports the manager's conclusion at the 5% level.

Exercise C (answers p. 99)

1   In a multiple-choice question paper of 120 questions, each with five possible answers, what number of correct answers would lead you to accept that a candidate was *not* answering purely by guesswork? To answer this question, set up appropriate null and alternative hypotheses and test at a 5% significance level.

2   3.141 592 653 589 79 ... shows the first fourteen decimal places of π. Is there any evidence to suggest that the number of even digits after the decimal point will be significantly different from the number of odd digits when the expansion is continued?

3   The breaking strain of a type of rope is Normally distributed with mean 1300 newtons and standard deviation 40 newtons. A sample of nine lengths gives the following results when tested.

> 1334,   1264,   1284,   1308,   1198,
>
> 1244,   1236,   1204,   1304 (newtons)

Is there evidence that the breaking strain is lower than expected and, if so, at what level of significance?

4   A machine produces ball-bearings whose diameters are Normally distributed with mean 3.00 mm and standard deviation 0.05 mm. A random sample of 50 ball-bearings is found to have mean 3.01 mm. Does the machine need adjusting?

5 A farmer grows cabbages under stable greenhouse conditions. Their weights are Normally distributed with mean 0.85 kg and variance 0.04 kg^2. One year he tries out a new fertiliser and weighs a random sample of 60 cabbages to see if there has been a significant improvement in yield. He finds that the 60 cabbages have a mean weight of 0.91 kg. Would you describe this evidence as 'significant', 'very significant' or 'highly significant'?

6 In a clinical trial, 1000 patients with a particular condition are given a new drug. Hospital records show that patients on existing treatments require surgery for their condition at an average rate of 14 operations per thousand patients per year. During the trial 6 of the patients receiving the new drug require surgery. The drug will only proceed to the next level of testing if the trial results provide evidence of a benefit to patients at the 1% level. Should the next level of testing go ahead? What would your answer be had only 5 operations been needed?

7 The number of items of luggage lost at a regional airport averages 100 per week. It is decided to employ a temporary baggage supervisor. In the third week following her appointment, only 70 items are lost. Using an appropriate distribution to model the number of items lost, provide a recommendation to the airport manager on whether or not to make the supervisor's appointment permanent.

After working through this chapter you should

1 understand the terms **null hypothesis** and **alternative hypothesis**

2 be familiar with the symbols H_0 and H_1

3 understand the meaning of a **type I error** and a **type II error**

4 understand what is meant by level of significance

5 know how to carry out a test of significance

6 know when to use a **one-tail test** and when to use a **two-tail test**.

Answers

1 Goodness of fit: the chi-squared test

A How good is a probabilistic model? (p. 1)

1D (a) Probabilistic model

(b) There is a great deal of uncertainty concerning the value of the pound and models to predict its value in the future need to assign probabilities to various possible outcomes. Models are therefore likely to be probabilistic, but once certain assumptions have been made, deterministic models may be used.

(c) Deterministic model

(d) Probabilistic model

(e) The rate of a nuclear reaction can be modelled with a deterministic mathematical model as it involves huge numbers of molecules and statistical fluctuations would 'even out'. The underlying process is again probabilistic

(f) Probabilistic model

2 The probability of throwing a one is $\frac{1}{6}$, so the expected number of ones is $\frac{1}{6} \times 1200 = 200$. Similarly, the expected number of sixes is also 200.

3 Dice A and C are possibly biased, but you cannot be sure. The results for dice B seem too good to be true! Dice D appears biased because the 'other' scores appear too low.

4 (a)

	1	6	Other
Observed	182	238	780
Expected	200	200	800
Deviation between O and E	−18	38	−20

Sum of deviations = 0

(b) This is not satisfactory as the positive and negative values cancel one another out.

5 (a) Dice A: $\Sigma(O - E)^2$
$$= 18^2 + 38^2 + 20^2 = 2168$$
Dice B: $\Sigma(O - E)^2 = 1^2 + 1^2 + 0^2 = 2$
Dice C: $\Sigma(O - E)^2$
$$= 20^2 + 18^2 + 38^2 = 2168$$
Dice D: $\Sigma(O - E)^2$
$$= 20^2 + 18^2 + 38^2 = 2168$$

(b) Comparing results for dice C and dice D gives the same value, but this calculation does not take into account the fact that dice D was only thrown 600 times, whereas dice C was thrown 1200 times.

(c) Comparing results for dice A and C also gives the same value, whereas, intuitively, you would expect different results.

6 (a) Dice B:
$$X^2 = \frac{(201 - 200)^2}{200} + \frac{(199 - 200)^2}{200}$$
$$+ \frac{(800 - 800)^2}{800} = 0.01$$
Dice C:
$$X^2 = \frac{(220 - 200)^2}{200} + \frac{(218 - 200)^2}{200}$$
$$+ \frac{(762 - 800)^2}{800} = 5.425$$
Dice D:
$$X^2 = \frac{(120 - 100)^2}{100} + \frac{(118 - 100)^2}{100}$$
$$+ \frac{(362 - 400)^2}{400} = 10.85$$

(b) In order of increasing value of X^2, the dice are B, C, A and D.

Exercise A (answers p. 5)

1 (a) (i) With $P(\text{boy}) = \frac{1}{2}$ the expected frequencies would be

	Boy first	Girl first
Boy second	25	25
Girl second	25	25

So $X^2 = \dfrac{(31-25)^2}{25} + \dfrac{(21-25)^2}{25}$

$+ \dfrac{(22-25)^2}{25} + \dfrac{(26-25)^2}{25}$

$= 2.48$

(ii) With P(boy) = 0.513 the expected frequencies would be

	Boy first	Girl first
Boy second	26.3	25.0
Girl second	25.0	23.7

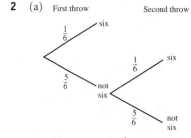

$100 \times P(GB) = 100 \times 0.487 \times 0.513 = 25.0$

$X^2 = \dfrac{(31-26.3)^2}{26.3} + \dfrac{(21-25)^2}{25}$

$+ \dfrac{(22-25)^2}{25} + \dfrac{(26-23.7)^2}{23.7}$

$= 2.06$

(b) Model (ii) fits these data better.

2 (a) First throw   Second throw

six

$\frac{1}{6}$

$\frac{5}{6}$ not six

$\frac{1}{6}$ six

$\frac{5}{6}$ not six

(i) $P(N=1) = \frac{1}{6}$
(ii) $P(N=2) = \frac{5}{6} \times \frac{1}{6}$
(iii) $P(N=3) = \frac{5}{6} \times \frac{5}{6} \times \frac{1}{6}$

(b)

N	1	2	3	4	5	6+
$P(N=n)$	0.167	0.139	0.116	0.096	0.080	0.402
Expected frequencies	33.4	27.8	23.2	19.2	16.0	80.4

(c) $X^2 = 4.5$

3 1560 books were loaned.

Expected number loaned per day

$= \dfrac{1560}{6} = 260$

$X^2 = \dfrac{(200-260)^2}{260} + \dfrac{(290-260)^2}{260} + \dots$

$= 20.6$

4 (a) A probability model for this situation would assume that:

- each coin was equally likely to come down head or tail;
- each trial was independent.

On this basis,

P(no heads in three cases)

$= \left(\frac{1}{2}\right)^3 = \frac{1}{8}$

In 800 such throws, the expected frequency is $800 \times \frac{1}{8} = 100$.

Similarly,

$P(1\ \text{head}) = \binom{3}{1}\left(\frac{1}{2}\right)\left(\frac{1}{2}\right)^2 = \frac{3}{8}$;

expected frequency = 300

$P(2\ \text{heads}) = \binom{3}{2}\left(\frac{1}{2}\right)^2\left(\frac{1}{2}\right) = \frac{3}{8}$;

expected frequency = 300

$P(3\ \text{heads}) = \left(\frac{1}{2}\right)^3 = \frac{1}{8}$;

expected frequency = 100

(b) $X^2 = 24.0$ (to 3 s.f.)

B   The chi-squared distribution (p. 6)

1 (a) 26.22   (b) 11.07

2 Dice B: $X^2 = 0.01$
Here there is almost perfect agreement between the proposed model and the 'real' data.

Dice C: $X^2 = 5.43$
The table indicates that a value higher than 4.61 would occur by chance in fewer than 10% of cases. Since the value obtained exceeds this you might conclude that the difference between the real data and the model of a fair dice is too great to have occurred by chance and the dice may be biased. Hence the result is significant at the 10% level.

Dice D: $X^2 = 10.85$
This is a high value. For a fair dice a value as great as or greater than 10.60 (from tables) would occur in only $\frac{1}{2}$% of all cases. This is a highly significant difference, significant at the 0.5% level. It is likely that this is not a fair dice.

3D The table of χ^2 probabilities tells us that, if dice B is unbiased, 90% of data collections should have $X^2 < 4.61$, but the shape of the χ^2 distribution indicates that $P(X^2 < \chi_p^2)$ for small values of χ_p^2 is very small indeed. Hence a very close fit may make us question whether the results are genuine, or have been fabricated to agree with the expected outcome.

Exercise B (p. 10)

1   (a) 2.5%   (b) 5%

2   (a) $a = 18.31$ (b) $c = 20.48$

C Testing a model: the chi-squared test (p. 10)

1   (a) Total number of girls
$= (1 \times 17) + (2 \times 21) + (3 \times 4) = 71$

(b) In 51 families which contain 3 children there will be a total of 153 children. The proportion of girls is therefore $\frac{71}{153} = 0.464$ (to 3 s.f.).

(c)

Number of girls per family	0	1	2	3
Probability	0.154	0.400	0.346	0.100
Expected frequency	7.85	20.4	17.65	5.1

2   (a) $X^2 = \dfrac{(9 - 7.85)^2}{7.85} + \dfrac{(17 - 20.4)^2}{20.4}$

$+ \dfrac{(21 - 17.65)^2}{17.65} + \dfrac{(4 - 5.1)^2}{5.1}$

$= 1.61$

(b) The lower value of X^2 suggests that this second model is a better fit than the binomial model with $p = 0.5$.

3

Number of girls	0	1	2	3
Observed	9	17	x	y

$9 + 17 + x + y = 51$
$x + y = 25$
$(0 \times 9) + (1 \times 17) + (2 \times x) + (3 \times y) = 71$
$2x + 3y = 54$
Solving for x and y gives $x = 21$ and $y = 4$.

Exercise C (p. 13)

1

Pea classification	RY	WY	RG	WG
O	55	20	16	9
E	56.25	18.75	18.75	6.25

W = wrinkled, R = round, Y = yellow, G = green

$X^2 = 1.72$

There are four cells, giving three degrees of freedom. $\chi^2 < 6.25$ in 90% of samples, so you can conclude that these results agree with Mendelian theory.

2 The proportion of imperfect peaches is 16%.

No. of imperfect peaches in box	0	1	2	3	4	5	6
Expected frequency	35.13	40.15	19.12	4.86	0.69	0.05	0

No. of imperfect peaches in box	0	1	2	3 or more
O	49	24	14	13
E	35.13	40.15	19.12	5.60

$X^2 = 23.12$ The number of degrees of freedom is two (p is calculated from the data, and the total number of peaches is also fixed).

$\chi^2(2) > 13.81$ in fewer than 0.1% of samples. The difference is highly significant (at the 0.1% level). The model used does not give a good fit with the data collected.

3   (a) $X^2 = 5.43$ with four degrees of freedom. The critical $\chi^2(4)$ value is 9.49 (at the 5% significance level). The differences are not significant and the B$(4, \frac{1}{2})$ model is appropriate for the data.

(b) $p = \frac{219}{400} = 0.5475$

You need to combine the 0 and 1 groups so that the expected frequency is greater than 5 for the cell. This gives $X^2 = 1.46$ with two degrees of freedom (4 cells – 2 constraints). The model fits the data.

Both distributions are acceptable models for the data.

D Contingency tables (p. 14)

1

	18–25	26–40	41–60	60+	Total
Will vote Labour	5.8	18.8	18.2	23.3	66
Will vote Conservative	13.2	43.2	41.8	53.7	152
Total		19	62	60	77	218

2 $X^2 = 7.75$

3 There are 3 degrees of freedom.
From $\chi^2(3)$ tables, $\chi^2(3)$ exceeds 6.25 for 10% of samples and it exceeds 7.81 for 5% of samples.

A value of 7.75 is therefore not significant at the 5% level.

There is no clear evidence in this sample to suggest that voting intention is related to age.

Exercise D (p. 17)

1 The model used assumes that there is no difference in grades awarded and gives the following table of expected grades.

	Grade				
	1	2	3	4	Total
College A	6.31	60.79	114.69	60.21	242
College B	4.69	45.21	85.31	44.79	180
Total	11	106	200	105	422

The results for grades 1 and 2 must be combined.

$X^2 = 1.54, \quad \nu = 2$

$\chi^2(2) < 4.61$ in 90% of samples.

There is no evidence that there is any significant difference in grades awarded by the two colleges.

2 The proportion of staff who are satisfied overall is $\frac{92}{190}$.

From this, the expected frequencies of all types of staff can be calculated.

	Satisfied	Not satisfied	Total
Doctors	34	36	70
Nurses	29	31	60
Ancillary staff	29	31	60
Total	92	98	190

The initial assumption is that job satisfaction is not related to the job done.

$X^2 = 34,$ number of degrees of freedom
$= (3 - 1)(2 - 1) = 2$

$\chi^2(2) > 13.81$ in less than 0.1% of samples. The evidence against the initial assumption is highly significant, suggesting that job satisfaction is related to job done.

3 An initial assumption that the drug is not effective would give the following expected frequency table.

	Drug	Placebo	Total
Improved	95.5	95.5	191
Not improved	104.5	104.5	209
Total	200	200	400

$X^2 = 21.20,$ degrees of freedom $= 1$

At the 1% level, $\chi^2 = 6.63$. Thus there is significant evidence to disprove the initial assumption and you can conclude that the drug is effective in improving the condition.

4 $X^2 = 7.04,$ degrees of freedom $= 1$

The difference in behaviour is significant at the 1% level.

2 Probability distributions for counting cases

A The geometric distribution (p. 20)

1
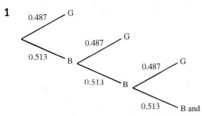

You must assume that the probabilities remain constant throughout – that each birth is independent of all other births.

2 (a) 0.487

   (b) $(0.513)(0.487) = 0.250$

   (c) $(0.513)^4(0.487) = 0.0337$

   (d) $(0.513)^{n-1}(0.487)$

3

x	1	2	3	4	5	6	7
$P(x)$	0.487	0.250	0.128	0.0657	0.0337	0.0173	0.008 88

4 $P(X \geqslant 8) = 1 - P(x < 8)$
$$= 1 - [P(X=1) + P(X=2) + \dots$$
$$+ P(X=7)]$$
$$= 0.009\ 35$$

Alternatively, if eight or more children are needed for the first girl, then the first seven must have been boys.

$P(7\ \text{boys}) = (0.513)^7 = 0.009\ 35$

5 (a) If $X = 1$ then the event occurs at the first trial. So $P(X=1) = p$

   (b) The event of interest occurs on the third trial. $P(X=3) = q \times q \times p = q^2 p$

   (c) $P(X=n) = \boxed{q \times q \times q \times \dots} \times p$
$$(n-1\ \text{non-occurrences})$$
$$= q^{n-1} p$$

Exercise A (p. 22)

1 (a) $P(X=3) = (0.8)^2(0.2) = 0.128$

   (b) $P(X<3) = P(X=1) + P(X=2)$
$$= 0.2 + (0.8)(0.2) = 0.36$$

   (c) $P(X \geqslant 3) = 1 - P(X<3) = 0.64$

2 Let X denote the number of trials until the right key is selected.

   (a) (i) $P(X=2) = \frac{3}{4} \times \frac{1}{3} = \frac{1}{4}$

      (ii) $P(X=4) = \frac{3}{4} \times \frac{2}{3} \times \frac{1}{2} = \frac{1}{4}$

   (b) $X \sim G(\frac{1}{4})$

      (i) $P(X=2) = \frac{3}{4} \times \frac{1}{4} = \frac{3}{16}$

      (ii) $P(X>2)$
$$= 1 - (P(X=1) + P(X=2))$$
$$= 1 - (\tfrac{1}{4} + \tfrac{3}{16}) = \tfrac{9}{16}$$

   (c) Both strategies are equally likely to succeed on the first trial, but the second strategy has higher probabilities of success after 2 or 3 trials (and guarantees success after the fourth).

3 (a) Let X denote the number of attempts required to pass. Then $X \sim G(0.4)$.
$$P(X=3) = (0.6)^2(0.4) = 0.144$$

   (b) $P(X>5) = 1 - P(X \leqslant 5)$
$$= 1 - [P(X=1) + P(X=2)$$
$$+ P(X=3) + P(X=4)$$
$$+ P(X=5)]$$
$$= 1 - [0.4 + (0.4)(0.6)$$
$$+ (0.4)(0.6)^2 + (0.4)(0.6)^3$$
$$+ (0.4)(0.6)^4]$$
$$= 1 - 0.922\ 24 = 0.077\ 76$$
or $P(X>5) = (0.6)^5 = 0.077\ 76$

4 (a) $(\frac{9}{10})^5 = 0\ 590\ 49$
$$= 0.59\ (\text{to 2 s.f.})$$

   (b) Having to select more than 20 digits to obtain the first zero means that all of the first 20 digits are non-zero.
$$P(20\ \text{non-zero digits}) = (\tfrac{9}{10})^{20}$$
$$= 0.122$$

B The binomial distribution revisited (p. 23)

1D The random variable (X) is the number of boys in the ten cots. X is a discrete variable which may take any of the values $0, 1, 2, \dots, 10$. On the assumption that babies are equally likely to be male or female, the appropriate binomial model for X is $X \sim B(10, \frac{1}{2})$.

2D As discussed in Section A the binomial and geometric variables have a number of factors in common. However, the geometric has an infinite number of possible outcomes, while for a binomial variable, the number of outcomes is finite. The geometric distribution counts the number of cases until an event occurs (including the occurrence of the event itself).

3 If X is the number of boys in the ward, then $X \sim B(10, \frac{1}{2})$.

$$P(X=1) = \binom{10}{1}\frac{1}{2} \times \left(\frac{1}{2}\right)^9$$

$$= \frac{10!}{9!1!}\left(\frac{1}{2}\right)^{10}$$

$$= 10(0.5)^{10}$$

$$= 0.0098 \text{ (to 2 s.f.)}$$

4E $P(X = r+1)$

$$= \frac{n!}{(r+1)!(n-r-1)!}p^{r+1}q^{n-r-1}$$

$$= \frac{n!(n-r)}{(r+1)r!(n-r)(n-r-1)!}pp^r q^{n-r}\frac{1}{q}$$

$$= \frac{n!}{(n-r)!r!}\left(\frac{n-r}{r+1}\right)\frac{p}{q}p^r q^{n-r}$$

$$= \left(\frac{n-r}{r+1}\right)\frac{p}{q}P(X=r)$$

5 (a)
(b)

x	0	1	2	3	
$P(X=x)$	0.42	0.42	0.14	0.02	

x	0	1	2	3	4
$P(X=x)$	0.20	0.40	0.30	0.10	0.01

Exercise B (p. 25)

1 X denotes the number of times the team won the toss.

$X \sim B(5, 0.5)$

(a) $P(X=3) = \binom{5}{3}(0.5)^2(0.5)^3$

$$= \frac{5!}{3!2!}(0.5)^5 = 0.3125$$

(b) $P(X \geqslant 3) = P(X=3) + P(X=4) + P(X=5)$

$$P(X=4) = \binom{5}{4}(0.5)^5 = 5(0.5)^5$$

$$= 0.156\ 25$$

$$P(X=5) = \binom{5}{5}(0.5)^5 = 0.031\ 25$$

$$\Rightarrow \quad P(X \geqslant 3) = 0.3125 + 0.156\ 25$$
$$+ 0.031\ 25 = 0.5$$

(This result could have been obtained by symmetry.)

2 $X \sim B(8, \frac{2}{3})$

$$P(X=0) = \left(\frac{1}{3}\right)^8 = 0.000\ 15$$

$$P(X=1) = \binom{8}{1}\left(\frac{2}{3}\right)\left(\frac{1}{3}\right)^7 = 0.002\ 44$$

Similarly,

$P(X=2) = 0.017\ 07$, $P(X=3) = 0.068\ 28$,
$P(X=4) = 0.170\ 71$, $P(X=5) = 0.273\ 13$,
$P(X=6) = 0.273\ 13$, $P(X=7) = 0.156\ 07$,
$P(X=8) = 0.039\ 02$

So 5 and 6 are the values which are most likely to occur.

3 You can approach this question by seeing how likely the outcome is if there is no preference for A or B.

Let X denote the number of people who prefer brand B. Then $X \sim B(6, 0.5)$.

$$P(X \geqslant 5) = \binom{6}{5}(0.5)(0.5)^5 + (0.5)^6$$

$$= 7(0.5)^6 = 0.1094$$

i.e. just over 1 in 10.

In practice this would not be considered to be sufficiently small to discard the assumption that A and B are equally well-liked.

4 Let X denote the number of correct questions.
Then $X \sim B(20, \frac{1}{3})$.

$P(X \geqslant 15) = 0.000\ 167$ (to 3 s.f.)

5E P(same number of heads on first 4 throws as last 4)

$$= \quad P(X=0,\ Y=0) + P(X=1,\ Y=1)$$
$$+ P(X=2,\ Y=2) + P(X=3,\ Y=3)$$
$$+ P(X=4,\ Y=4)$$

(where X and Y denote the number of heads on the first and last four throws respectively)

$$= [(0.5)^4]^2 + [4(0.5)^4]^2 + \left[\binom{4}{2}(0.5)^4\right]^2$$

$$+ \left[\binom{4}{3}(0.5)^4\right]^2 + [(0.5)^4]^2$$

$$= 0.273$$

By symmetry, the probability that there are more tails on the first four throws than the last four $= \dfrac{1 - 0.273}{2} = 0.36$ (to 2 s.f.)

C The Poisson distribution (p. 25)

1D Theoretically, X can take any whole-number value, although large numbers will be very unlikely. The distribution could not be binomial as it has the possibility of infinitely many outcomes. The distribution is not geometric as it is not waiting for an event to happen.

2 (a) The mean of $B(n, p)$ is np.
$np = 12 \times \frac{1}{3} = 4$

(b)

x	0	1	2	3	4	5	6
$P(X = x)$	0.008	0.046	0.127	0.212	0.238	0.191	0.111

x	7	8	9	10	11	12
$P(X = x)$	0.048	0.015	0.003	0.000	0.000	0.000

3 (a) There are 48 intervals of 15 minutes. On average, there are four requests in 12 hours.

P(request in a 15-minute interval)
$= \frac{4}{48} = \frac{1}{12}$

(b) $X \sim B(48, \frac{1}{12})$

(c)

x	0	1	2	3	4	5	6
$P(X = x)$	0.015	0.067	0.143	0.199	0.204	0.163	0.106

x	7	8	9	10	11	12
$P(X = x)$	0.058	0.027	0.011	0.004	0.001	0.000

4 $X \sim B(720, \frac{1}{180})$

x	0	1	2	3	4	5	6
$P(X = x)$	0.018	0.073	0.146	0.196	0.196	0.157	0.104

x	7	8	9	10	11	12
$P(X = x)$	0.060	0.030	0.013	0.005	0.002	0.001

5 $X \sim B(7200, \frac{1}{1800})$

x	0	1	2	3	4	5	6
$P(X = x)$	0.018	0.073	0.147	0.195	0.195	0.156	0.104

x	7	8	9	10	11	12
$P(X = x)$	0.060	0.030	0.013	0.005	0.002	0.001

6 np is the mean value.
For $X \sim B(48, \frac{1}{12})$ the mean is $48 \times \frac{1}{12} = 4$.
Similarly, $np = 4$ for the other distributions.

7 The 4 represents the mean number of requests.
In the general expression for $P(X = r)$,

$$P(X = r) = \frac{e^{-\lambda}\lambda^{r}}{r!} \text{ where } \lambda \text{ is the mean value}$$

8 $P(X = 0) = \dfrac{e^{-4}4^{0}}{0!} = e^{-4} = 0.0183$

$P(X = 1) = \dfrac{e^{-4}4^{1}}{1} = 4e^{-4} = 0.073$

$P(X = 2) = \dfrac{e^{-4}4^{2}}{2!} = 0.147$

and so on.

Your results should confirm that the distributions are identical and that the given distribution provides a very good approximation to the binomial under the conditions indicated.

9 $P(X \geqslant 4) = 1 - P(X < 4)$
$= 1 - P(X = 0, 1, 2, 3)$
$P(X = 0) = e^{-4} = 0.0183$
$P(X = 1) = 4e^{-4} = 0.073$
$P(X = 2) = \dfrac{4^{2}e^{-4}}{2!} = 0.147$
$P(X = 3) = \dfrac{4^{3}e^{-4}}{3!} = 0.195$
$P(X \geqslant 4) = 0.567$

Exercise C (p. 29)

1 (a) 2

(b) (i) $P(0) = \dbinom{100}{0}(0.02)^{0}(0.98)^{100}$
$= (0.98)^{100} = 0.133$ (to 3 s.f.)

(ii) P(at least one) $= 1 - P(0)$
$= 0.867$ (to 3 s.f.)

(c) Mean $= np = 2$
$P(0) = e^{-2} = 0.135$ (to 3 s.f.)
P(at least one) $= 1 - 0.135$
$= 0.865$ (to 3 s.f.)

2 (a) 0.006 74 (b) 0.0842
(c) 0.960 (to 3 s.f.)

3 (a) $P(0) = e^{-1.4} = 0.247$ (to 3 s.f.)

(b) $\qquad$ P(2 or more) $= 1 - P(0) - P(1)$
$P(1) = 1.4e^{-1.4}$
$\Rightarrow$ P(2 or more) $= 0.408$ (to 3 s.f.)

4 Let X be the number of customers arriving at the check-out in one minute.

$$X \sim P(2.4)$$
$$P(X > 3) = 0.221 \quad \text{(to 3 s.f.)}$$

5 0.549, 0.329, 0.099, 0.020

6 0.323

7 0.125

8 0.185

D From binomial to Poisson (p. 30)

1E $P(X = r + 1) = \dfrac{e^{-\lambda} \lambda^{r+1}}{(r+1)!}$

$$= \frac{\lambda}{(r+1)} \frac{e^{-\lambda} \lambda^r}{r!} = \frac{\lambda}{r+1} P(X = r)$$

$$P(X = 0) = \frac{e^{-\lambda} \lambda^0}{0!} = e^{-\lambda}$$

2E $e^{-\lambda} = 1 - \dfrac{\lambda}{1!} + \dfrac{\lambda^2}{2!} - \dfrac{\lambda^3}{3!} + \ldots$

3E Define $\lambda = np$, so $p = \dfrac{\lambda}{n}$.

Now $q = 1 - p$, so $q^n = \left(1 - \dfrac{\lambda}{n}\right)^n$

$$\Rightarrow \quad q^n = 1 - \frac{n\lambda}{n} + \binom{n}{2} \frac{\lambda^2}{n^2} - \binom{n}{3} \frac{\lambda^3}{n^3} + \ldots$$

$$= 1 - \lambda + \frac{n(n-1)}{2!} \frac{\lambda^2}{n^2}$$

$$- \frac{n(n-1)(n-2)}{3!} \frac{\lambda^3}{n^3} + \ldots$$

$$= 1 - \lambda + \frac{\lambda^2}{2!}\left(1 - \frac{1}{n}\right)$$

$$- \frac{\lambda^3}{3!}\left(1 - \frac{1}{n}\right)\left(1 - \frac{2}{n}\right) + \ldots$$

4E As $n \to \infty$, $\left(1 - \dfrac{1}{n}\right) \to 1$, $\left(1 - \dfrac{2}{n}\right) \to 1$

and so on.

Then $q^n \to 1 - \lambda + \dfrac{\lambda^2}{2!} - \dfrac{\lambda^3}{3!} + \ldots$

i.e. $q^n \to e^{-\lambda}$

5E $\dfrac{(n-r)p}{q} = \dfrac{\left(1 - \dfrac{r}{n}\right)np}{q} = \dfrac{\left(1 - \dfrac{r}{n}\right)\lambda}{q}$

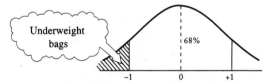

$$= \frac{\left(1 - \dfrac{r}{n}\right)\lambda}{1 - p} = \frac{\left(1 - \dfrac{r}{n}\right)\lambda}{1 - \dfrac{\lambda}{n}}$$

$$\Rightarrow \quad \text{as } n \to \infty, \frac{(n-r)p}{1} \to \lambda$$

so $\dfrac{(n-r)p}{(r+1)q} \to \dfrac{\lambda}{r+1}$

3 Continuous random variables

A The Normal probability density function (p. 32)

It is useful to be able to make approximate calculations with the Normal distribution based on the knowledge that 68% of the values should be within one standard deviation of the mean and 98% within two standard deviations. Recall also that a sketch always helps in solving problems on the Normal distribution.

1D (a) Underweight bags are at least one standard deviation below the mean.

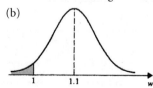

So 32% (approximately) are more than one standard deviation away from the mean, with 16% beyond +1 and 16% below −1 standard deviation.

About 16% of bags are underweight.

(b)

About 16% of bags are underweight.

Let W = weight of sugar

$$z = \frac{1 - 1.1}{0.1} = -1$$

$$P(W < 1.0 \text{ kg}) = \Phi(-1)$$

$$= 1 - \Phi(1)$$

$$= 1 - 0.8413$$

$$= 15.9\% \quad \text{(to 3 s.f.)}$$

Exercise A (p. 34)

1 Let the total journey time be T minutes.

$$T \sim N(20, 5^2)$$

$P(T > 26)$ is required.

Standardising, $z = \dfrac{26 - 20}{5} = 1.2$

$$P(T > 26) = 1 - \Phi(1.2)$$

$$= 1 - 0.885 \quad \text{(from tables)}$$

$$= 0.115$$

I will be late on about 12% of journeys.

2 (a) 0.726   (b) 0.104

3 The standard deviation is about 4.4 days.

4 0.22

B General probability density functions (p. 34)

1D $f(x) \geq 0$ for all x because $f(x)$ determines *probabilities*, which must always be greater than or equal to 0 (and less than or equal to 1).

The total area under the graph of $f(x)$,

$\displaystyle\int_{-\infty}^{\infty} f(x)\,dx$, represents the probability that

one of the X values occurs. Since the probability is 1 that *some* value will occur,

$\displaystyle\int_{-\infty}^{\infty} f(x)\,dx$ *must* equal 1.

2 $P(\text{symptoms on 1st day}) = \displaystyle\int_0^1 f(x)\,dx$

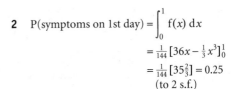

$$= \tfrac{1}{144}[36x - \tfrac{1}{3}x^3]_0^1$$

$$= \tfrac{1}{144}[35\tfrac{2}{3}] = 0.25$$

$$\text{(to 2 s.f.)}$$

Exercise B (p. 36)

1 (a) $0 \leq X \leq 3$

(b)

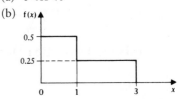

Area under $f(x) = 1 \times \tfrac{1}{2} + 2 \times \tfrac{1}{4} = 1$

(c) (i) $P(X \geq 1) = \tfrac{1}{2}$

(ii) $P(X \geq \tfrac{1}{2}) = \tfrac{3}{4}$

(iii) $P(\tfrac{1}{2} \leq X \leq 2) = \tfrac{1}{2}$

(iv) $P(X \leq 3) = 1$

2 (a) The area under the curve must equal 1.

Area of triangle $= \tfrac{1}{2}$ base $\times$ height

$$= \tfrac{1}{2} \times 2 \times k = k$$

$$\Rightarrow \quad k = 1$$

(b) (i) $P(X \geq 1.5) = 0.125$

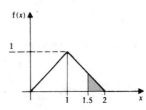

(ii) $P(X \leq 0.5) = 0.125$

(iii) $P(0.5 \leq X \leq 1.5) = 0.75$

3 $0 \leq X \leq 10$ and $f(x) = 0.0012x^2(10 - x)$

(a) $P(X > 5) = \displaystyle\int_5^{10} f(x)\,dx$

$$= 0.0012 \int_5^{10} x^2(10 - x)\,dx$$

$$= 0.0012[\tfrac{10}{3}x^3 - \tfrac{1}{4}x^4]_5^{10}$$

$$= 0.0012[(833.3) - (260.4)]$$

$$= 0.687 \quad \text{(to 3 s.f.)}$$

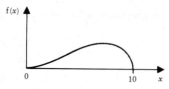

(b) $P(1 < X < 2) = \int_1^2 f(x)\, dx$

$$= 0.0012[\tfrac{10}{3} x^3 - \tfrac{1}{4} x^4]_1^2$$

$$= 0.0235$$

C Cumulative distribution functions
(p. 36)

Exercise C (p. 37)

1 (a) $\int_a^b f(x)\, dx = 1$

therefore $[kx]_a^b = 1$

$k(b-a) = 1$

$$k = \frac{1}{b-a}$$

(b) $F(t) = \int_a^t f(x)\, dx = [kx]_a^t$

$$= kt - ka = \frac{t-a}{b-a} \text{ for } a \leqslant t \leqslant b$$

2 (a) $F(5) = 1 - \tfrac{1}{5} = \tfrac{4}{5}$

(b) Required probability
$= F(4) - F(2) = (1 - \tfrac{1}{4}) - (1 - \tfrac{1}{2}) = \tfrac{1}{4}$

(c) $f(t) = \dfrac{d}{dt} F(t) = \dfrac{1}{t^2} \text{ for } t \geqslant 1$

D The mean, variance and other measures of variability (p. 38)

Exercise D (p. 41)

1 (a) $1 = \int_0^1 kx^2\, dx$

$$= k[\tfrac{1}{3} x^3]_0^1 = k(\tfrac{1}{3} - 0)$$

$$\Rightarrow \quad k = 3$$

(b) $\mu = \int_0^1 xf(x)\, dx$

$$= 3 \int_0^1 x^3\, dx$$

$$= 3[\tfrac{1}{4} x^4]_0^1$$

$$= 3(\tfrac{1}{4} - 0) = \tfrac{3}{4}$$

$$\sigma^2 = \int_0^1 x^2 f(x)\, dx - \mu^2$$

$$= 3 \int_0^1 x^2 x^2\, dx - (\tfrac{3}{4})^2$$

$$= 3[\tfrac{1}{5} x^5]_0^1 - (\tfrac{3}{4})^2$$

$$\Rightarrow \quad \sigma^2 = \tfrac{3}{5} - (\tfrac{3}{4})^2 = 0.0375$$

(c) $P(X \geqslant 0.5) = 3 \int_{0.5}^1 x^2\, dx$

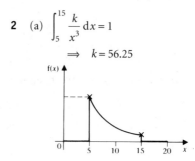

$$= 3[\tfrac{1}{3} x^3]_{0.5}^1$$

$$= 1 - 0.5^3 = 0.875$$

2 (a) $\int_5^{15} \dfrac{k}{x^3}\, dx = 1$

$$\Rightarrow \quad k = 56.25$$

(b) $\mu = 7.5$

(c)

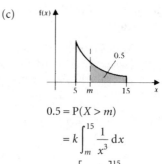

$$0.5 = P(X > m)$$

$$= k \int_m^{15} \frac{1}{x^3}\, dx$$

$$= k \left[-\frac{1}{2x^2} \right]_m^{15}$$

$$= \frac{k}{2}\left[\left(-\frac{1}{15^2}\right) - \left(-\frac{1}{m^2}\right) \right]$$

$$\Rightarrow \quad m^2 = 45$$

$$\Rightarrow \quad m = 6.71$$

3
$$\mu = \int_0^{10} x f(x) \, dx$$

$$= 0.0012 \int_0^{10} x^3(10 - x) \, dx$$

$$= 0.0012 \int_0^{10} (10x^3 - x^4) \, dx$$

$$= 0.0012[\tfrac{10}{4} x^4 - \tfrac{1}{5} x^5]_0^{10}$$

$$\implies \mu = 6$$

The mean distance travelled is 6 metres.

4 (b) $m = 1.45$ (c) 0.450

5 (a) $k = -6$

(b) The graph of $f(x)$ is symmetric; the median divides the area under $f(x)$ into two equal portions.

(c) 0.156

6 $f(x) = \dfrac{dF(x)}{dx}$, so

$$f(x) = \begin{cases} 0 & \text{for} & x < 0 \\ \tfrac{1}{4} & \text{for} & 0 \leqslant x < 1 \\ \tfrac{1}{2} & \text{for} & 1 \leqslant x < 2 \\ \tfrac{1}{4} & \text{for} & 2 \leqslant x < 3 \\ 0 & \text{for} & 3 \leqslant x \end{cases}$$

$F(x) = 0.95 \implies \tfrac{1}{4}(x+1) = 0.95$

$$\implies x + 1 \quad = 3.8$$

$$\implies x \qquad = 2.8$$

So the 95th percentile is 2.8

$F(x) = 0.05 \implies \tfrac{1}{4} x = 0.05$

$$\implies x \quad = 0.2$$

So the 5th percentile is 0.2

4 Selecting and testing the models

A Choosing a suitable model (p. 44)

1D (a) It is not binomial as there is no fixed value for n, the number of trials. It is not Poisson as X cannot equal 0 and the events do not occur over a continuous interval of time. The geometric distribution is the most suitable as it is measuring the number of trials before an event occurs.

(b) To use the geometric distribution, you must assume that successive attempts are independent.

2 (a) Binomial. Assume each dice is independent.
$$X \sim B(5, \tfrac{1}{6})$$

(b) Geometric. Assume independence.
$$X \sim G(\tfrac{1}{6})$$

(c) Binomial. Assume births are independent.
$$X \sim B(4, 0.5) \text{ or } X \sim B(4, 0.513)$$
assuming that $P(\text{boy}) = 0.513$ as stated on page 20.

(d) Poisson. Assume radioactive emissions occur randomly, singly and independently. λ would be defined as the average number of emissions in a five-second interval.

(e) Geometric. To specify the model in further detail you need to know the probability of a goal being scored in a home match.

Exercise A (p. 45)

1 (a) The binomial distribution is a possible model as each event has two possible outcomes (boy or girl) and births can be regarded as being independent. If it is assumed that boys and girls are equally likely outcomes, then $p = \tfrac{1}{2}$. As there are five children in each family, $n = 5$.

(b)

		Expected values
$P(X=0) =$	$(\tfrac{1}{2})^5 = 0.031\,25$	$300 \times P(X=0) = 9.375$
$P(X=1) =$	$5(\tfrac{1}{2})^5 = 0.156\,25$	$300 \times P(X=1) = 46.875$
$P(X=2) =$	$10(\tfrac{1}{2})^5 = 0.3125$	$300 \times P(X=2) = 93.75$
$P(X=3) =$	$10(\tfrac{1}{2})^5 = 0.3125$	$300 \times P(X=3) = 93.75$
$P(X=4) =$	$5(\tfrac{1}{2})^5 = 0.156\,25$	$300 \times P(X=4) = 46.875$
$P(X=5) =$	$(\tfrac{1}{2})^5 = 0.031\,25$	$300 \times P(X=5) = 9.375$

$$X^2 = \sum \frac{(O - E)^2}{E} = 11.04$$

There are six cells and therefore five degrees of freedom.

$\chi^2(5) = 11.07$ at the 5% level

So there is insufficient evidence to reject the model.

(c) Number of boys $= 809$
     Number of children $= 1500$

So $p = \dfrac{809}{1500}$. Put $q = 1 - p$.

		Expected values
$P(X = 0) = q^5$	$= 0.021$	6.22
$P(X = 1) = 5pq^4$	$= 0.121$	36.43
$P(X = 2) = 10p^2 q^3$	$= 0.284$	85.31
$P(X = 3) = 10p^3 q^2$	$= 0.333$	99.88
$P(X = 4) = 5p^4 q$	$= 0.195$	58.47
$P(X = 5) = p^5$	$= 0.046$	13.69

$X^2 = 1.137$

$\chi^2(4) = 9.49$ at the 5% level

The fit appears to be much better. Note that there are only four degrees of freedom as there are two constraints. p is estimated from the data and the total is the same for both expected and observed frequencies.

(d) The second model gives the best fit. You would expect this as p is estimated from the data.

2 (a) N has a binomial distribution as it has only two possible outcomes (point up or down) and you can assume that each drawing pin lands independently of the others.

(b) (i) Number of pins
          landing point up $=$ 690
          Number of trials $=$ 1200
          So an estimate of p is $\frac{690}{1200}$ $= 0.575$

(ii) Assume $N \sim B(4, p)$.

		Expected values
$P(N = 0) = q^4$	$= 0.033$	9.79
$P(N = 1) = 4pq^3$	$= 0.177$	52.97
$P(N = 2) = 6p^2 q^2$	$= 0.358$	107.49
$P(N = 3) = 4p^3 q$	$= 0.323$	96.96
$P(N = 4) = p^4$	$= 0.109$	32.79

$X^2 = 3.5$

There are three degrees of freedom (5 cells – 2 constraints). $\chi^2(3) = 7.81$ at the 5% level So the model is suitable.

B The geometric distribution as a model (p. 46)

1 For 200 trials, you would expect results *similar* to

1	2	3	4	...
20	18	16	15	...

2 You must assume that successive numbers are independent. There are 10 possible outcomes. If the numbers are chosen at random then each is equally likely and so
$P(\text{zero is chosen}) = \frac{1}{10}$.

3 You will find it necessary to group a number of cells. The more data you collect, the better.

4 For your data you should calculate
$$\frac{\text{total number of runs of length one}}{\text{total number of trials}}$$

5 The second model should be a better fit as p is generated using *all* the data.

6 The mean run length for your data should be approximately 10.

C Fitting a Poisson distribution to data (p. 48)

Exercise C (p. 49)

1 (a) $\bar{x} = \text{mean} = \dfrac{81}{60} = 1.35$

$\text{Variance} = \dfrac{1}{n} (\Sigma\, x^2) - \bar{x}^2 = 1.19$
                                              (to 3 s.f.)

(b) You can consider the arrival of customers as random and independent and the variance as close to the mean.

2 (a) As the disease is not known to be infectious, you can assume that each outbreak is random and independent. Since the values of the mean, 1.26, and variance, 1.57, are reasonably close, a Poisson model is reasonable.

(b)

X	0	1	2	3	4	5	6	7
P(X)	0.28	0.36	0.23	0.09	0.03	0.008	0.002	0.0003
E	28.4	35.7	22.5	9.46	2.98	0.75	0.16	0.028

13.4

Group these cells together to make the expected frequency greater than 5.

(c) $\sum \dfrac{(O-E)^2}{E} = 0.341$

There are 4 cells and 2 constraints, giving 2 degrees of freedom.

$\chi^2(2) = 5.99$ at the 5% level

The model is a good fit.

3   (a) $\lambda =$ mean $= 9.4$ Variance $= 10.2$

(b) Regroup the data to avoid having expected numbers smaller than 5.

Number of water fleas	0 to 6	7	8	9	10	11	12 or more
Probability	0.173	0.106	0.125	0.131	0.123	0.105	0.237
Expected	8.64	5.32	6.25	6.53	6.14	5.25	11.87
Observed	8	6	7	4	5	7	13

$\sum \dfrac{(O-E)^2}{E} = 2.11$

There are 7 cells and 2 constraints, so there are 5 degrees of freedom.

$\chi^2(5) = 11.07$ (at the 5% level)

The model appears to be a good fit.

4   228, 211, 98, 30, 7, 2 (for 5 or more).

$X^2 = 1.2$

d.f. $= 3$ (you need to combine 2 groups)
The differences are not significant.

5   (a) $\lambda = \dfrac{196}{280} = 0.7$

(b)

	E	
$P(X=0) = 0.497$	139.0	
$P(X=1) = 0.348$	97.3	
$P(X=2) = 0.122$	34.1	
$P(X=3) = 0.028$	7.95	
$P(X=4) = 0.005$	1.39	9.60
$P(X \geqslant 5) = 0.0007$	0.26	

The fit appears to be reasonable.

(c) $\sum \dfrac{(O-E)^2}{E} = 1.92$

There are 4 cells with 2 constraints, so there are 2 degrees of freedom.

$\chi^2(2) = 5.99$ at the 5% level, suggesting that the model is satisfactory.

D   The Normal distribution as an approximation to the Poisson distribution (p. 51)

1   For the Poisson distribution P(30),

$$P(25 \leqslant X \leqslant 30) = \frac{30^{25}e^{-30}}{25!} + \frac{30^{26}e^{-30}}{26!}$$

$$+ \dots + \frac{30^{30}e^{-30}}{30!}$$

$$= 0.39$$

For the Normal distribution N(30, 30),

$P(24.5 < X \leqslant 30.5)$

$$= P\left(\frac{24.5 - 30}{\sqrt{30}} < Z \leqslant \frac{30.5 - 30}{\sqrt{30}}\right)$$

$$= \Phi(0.091) - (1 - \Phi(1.004))$$

$$= 0.5363 + 0.8423 - 1$$

$$= 0.38$$

Exercise D (p. 53)

1   Using N(50, 50),

$$P(X \leqslant 45.5) = P\left(z \leqslant \frac{45.5 - 50}{\sqrt{50}}\right)$$

$$= 1 - P(z \leqslant 0.636)$$

$$= 1 - \Phi(0.636)$$

$$= 1 - 0.738$$

$$= 0.262$$

2   The number of fans replaced in a month has a Poisson distribution with $\lambda = 20$. This can be approximated by N(20, 20). Using tables, $\Phi(0.675) = 0.75$, so there is a probability of 0.75 that the number of fans replaced in any month will be less than $20 + 0.675 \times 20 = 33.5$.

The engineer should have 34 fans in stock.

5 Forming new variables

A Combining random variables (p. 94)

1 (a) $P(Y + B = 5) = P(Y_4, B_1) + P(Y_3, B_2)$
$+ P(Y_2, B_3)$
$= 0.1 \times 0.25 + 0.2 \times 0.5$
$+ 0.3 \times 0.25 = 0.20$

$P(2) = P(Y_1, B_1) = 0.10$

$P(4) = P(Y_2, B_2) + P(Y_3, B_1)$
$+ P(Y_1, B_3) = 0.30$

$P(7) = P(Y_4, B_3) = 0.025$

Score $Y + B$	Probability
2	0.1
3	0.275
4	0.3
5	0.2
6	0.1
7	0.025

(b) Mean$(Y + B) = 4.0$

Variance$(Y + B) = 1.5$

Note that

mean$(Y + B) =$ mean$(Y) +$ mean(B)

and variance$(Y + B)$

$=$ variance$(Y) +$ variance(B)

2

$2b$	2	4	6
P($2b$)	0.25	0.5	0.25

Mean$(2B) = 2 \times 0.25 + 4 \times 0.5 + 6 \times 0.25$
$= 4 = 2$ mean(B)

Variance$(2B) = 2 = 2^2$ variance(B)

$3y$	3	6	9	12
P($3y$)	0.4	0.3	0.2	0.1

Mean$(3Y) = 6 = 3$ mean(Y)

Variance$(3Y) = 9 = 3^2$ variance(Y)

3

Score on dice (D)	1	2	3	4	5	6
Probability	$\frac{1}{6}$	$\frac{1}{6}$	$\frac{1}{6}$	$\frac{1}{6}$	$\frac{1}{6}$	$\frac{1}{6}$

Mean$(D) = \frac{1}{6}(1 + 2 + 3 + 4 + 5 + 6)$
$= 3.5$

Variance(D)
$= \frac{1}{6}(1^2 + 2^2 + 3^2 + 4^2 + 5^2 + 6^2) - (3.5)^2$
≈ 2.9

Option 1

Mean$(D_1 + D_2) = 2$ mean$(D) = 7$

Variance$(D_1 + D_2)$
$=$ variance$(D) +$ variance(D)
$= 2$ variance$(D) \approx 5.8$

Option 2

Mean$(2D) = 2$ mean$(D) = 7$

Variance$(2D) = 2^2$ variance(D)
$= 4$ variance$(D) \approx 11.7$

The expected winnings are the same for each option. Your prize money would be 7p minus the cost to play. If it cost less than 7p per go, then you would expect (in the long term) to win on both options.

The variance (variability) is much greater with option 2. You have a chance of winning (or losing) more per go.

More cautious players might prefer option 1!

4 (a)

$A - B$	-2	-1	0	1
P($A - B$)	0.1	0.4	0.4	0.1

(b) Mean$(A) = 1$
Mean$(B) = 1.5$

Variance$(A) = 0.4$
Variance$(B) = 0.25$

Mean$(A - B) = -0.5$
$=$ Mean$(A) -$ Mean(B)

Variance$(A - B) = 0.65$
$=$ Variance$(A) +$ Variance(B)

Exercise A (p. 58)

1

x	1	2	5	8
$P(X = x)$	$\frac{1}{4}$	$\frac{1}{4}$	$\frac{1}{4}$	$\frac{1}{4}$

(a) (i) Mean(X)

$$= (1 \times \tfrac{1}{4}) + (2 \times \tfrac{1}{4}) + (5 \times \tfrac{1}{4})$$
$$+ (8 \times \tfrac{1}{4})$$
$$= \tfrac{1}{4} \times 16 = 4$$

(ii) Variance(X)

$$= (1^2 \times \tfrac{1}{4}) + (2^2 \times \tfrac{1}{4}) + (5^2 \times \tfrac{1}{4})$$
$$+ (8^2 \times \tfrac{1}{4}) - 4^2$$
$$= \tfrac{1}{4}(1 + 4 + 25 + 64) - 16$$
$$= \tfrac{94}{4} - 16 = 7.5$$

(b) Mean($2X$) = 2 mean(X) = $2 \times 4 = 8$

Variance($2X$) = 4V(X)

$$= 4 \times 7.5 = 30$$

(c) Mean($3X$) = 3 mean(X) = $3 \times 4 = 12$

V($3X$) = 9V(X)

$$= 9 \times 7.5 = 67.5$$

(d) Mean($X_1 + X_2$) = mean(X_1)
$$+ \text{mean}(X_2)$$
$$= 2 \text{ mean}(X) = 8$$

Variance($X_1 + X_2$) = V(X_1) + V(X_2)
$$= 2\text{V}(X) = 15$$

2

x	1	2	3	4
$P(X = x)$	$\frac{1}{6}$	$\frac{2}{6}$	$\frac{2}{6}$	$\frac{1}{6}$

(a) Mean = 2.5   Variance = 0.917

(b) Mean($2X$) = 2 mean(X) = 5

Variance($2X$) = 4V(X) ≈ 3.7

(c) Mean($X_1 + 2X_2$) = 7.5

Variance($X_1 + 2X_2$) ≈ 4.6

3 (a) $\frac{20}{3}$ (b) $\frac{80}{3}$ (c) $\frac{40}{3}$ (d) $\frac{100}{3}$

4 (a) $Y = -1 \Rightarrow (X_1, X_2, X_3) = (-1, -1, -1)$

or $(-1, -1, 0)$ (in any order)

or $(-1, -1, 1)$ (in any order)

Adding probabilities

$$\Rightarrow \quad P(Y = -1) = 0.104$$

The distribution of Y is symmetrical
and therefore

$$P(Y = 1) = 0.104 \quad P(Y = 0) = 0.792$$

(b) Mean(Y) = 0   Variance(Y) = 0.208

B   Combining Poisson variables (p. 59)

Exercise B (p. 60)

1 (a) Mean($X + Y$) = mean(X)
$$+ \text{mean}(Y) = 7$$

(b) $X + Y \sim P(7)$

$P(X + Y < 4) = 0.0818$

2 (a) $X \sim P(3)$ Mean(X) = 3

Variance(X) = 3

$Y \sim P(2)$ Mean(Y) = 2

Variance(Y) = 2

Mean($X + Y$) = $3 + 2 = 5$

Variance($X + Y$) = $3 + 2 = 5$

(b) $X + Y \sim P(5)$

(i) 0.007   (ii) 0.875

3 (a) (i) 0.008   (ii) 0.857

(b) 0.046

C   Expectation and variance (p. 60)

1 (a) $X = x_1, x_2, \ldots, x_i, \ldots, x_n$

$aX = ax_1, ax_2, \ldots$

$$E[aX] = \sum_{i=1}^{n} ax_i P(x_i)$$
$$= a \sum_{1}^{n} x_i P(x_i) = aE[X]$$

(b) $$E[X + b] = \sum_{1}^{n} (x_i + b)P(x_i)$$
$$= \sum_{1}^{n} x_i P(x_i) + b \sum_{1}^{n} P(x_i)$$
$$= E[X] + b$$

(c) $$V[aX] = E[a^2 X^2] - (E[aX])^2$$
$$= a^2 E[X^2] - a^2(E[X])^2$$
$$= a^2\{E[X^2] - (E[X])^2\}$$
$$= a^2 V[X]$$

2E $(x_1 + y_1), (x_1 + y_2), (x_2 + y_1), (x_2 + y_2),$
$(x_3 + y_1), (x_3 + y_2)$

3E (a) $P(x_1) = P(x_1 y_1 \text{ or } x_1 y_2)$
$$= P(x_1 y_1) + P(x_1 y_2)$$

$a = r + u$

(b) $P(y_1) = P(y_1x_1 \text{ or } y_1x_2 \text{ or } y_1x_3)$
$$= P(y_1x_1) + P(y_1x_2) + P(y_1x_3)$$
$$d = r + s + t$$

(c) y_1 or y_2 must occur in the sum $X + Y$, hence $P(y_1 \text{ or } y_2) = 1$.

4E $E[XY] = (x_1y_1)r + (x_1y_2)u + (x_2y_1)s$
$$+ (x_2y_2)v + (x_3y_1)t$$
$$+ (x_3y_2)w \qquad (1)$$

But $r = P(x_1y_1) = P(x_1)P(y_1)$
as X and Y are independent
$$= ad$$

Similarly for the other probabilities, i.e. $s = bd$, $t = cd$ etc.
So equation (1) becomes

$E[XY] = (x_1y_1)ad + (x_1y_1)ae + \dots$
$$= (x_1a)(y_1d) + (x_1a)(y_1e) + \dots$$
$$= (x_1a)(y_1d + y_1e)$$
$$+ (x_2b)(y_1d + y_1e) + \dots$$
$$= (x_1a)(E[Y]) + (x_2b)(E[Y])$$
$$+ (x_3c)(E[Y])$$
$$= E[X]E[Y]$$

5 $E[X] = \int_0^1 x\,dx = 0.5$

$E[Y] = \int_0^{0.5} 2y\,dy = 0.25$

$E[X + Y] = E[X] + E[Y] = 0.75$

6 $E[T] = \int_1^5 \dfrac{5}{4}\dfrac{t}{t^2}\,dt = \tfrac{5}{4}[\ln t]_1^5 = \tfrac{5}{4}\ln 5 = 2.01$

$V[T] = E[T^2] - (E[T])^2$
$$= \int_1^5 \dfrac{5}{4}\dfrac{t^2}{t^2}\,dt - 2.01^2$$
$$= \tfrac{5}{4}[t]_1^5 - 2.01^2$$
$$= 5 - 4.04$$
$$= 0.96$$

7 $E[X] = \int_0^2 \tfrac{1}{2}x^2\,dx = \tfrac{1}{6}[x^3]_0^2 = \tfrac{4}{3}$

$V[X] = \int_0^2 \tfrac{1}{2}x^3\,dx - (\tfrac{4}{3})^2$
$$= \tfrac{1}{8}[x^4]_0^2 - (\tfrac{4}{3})^2$$
$$= \tfrac{2}{9}$$

$E[Y] = \int_0^{\frac{1}{2}} 2y\,dy = [y^2]_0^{\frac{1}{2}} = \tfrac{1}{4}$

$V[Y] = \int_0^{\frac{1}{2}} 2y^2\,dy - (\tfrac{1}{4})^2$
$$= \tfrac{2}{3}[y^3]_0^{\frac{1}{2}} - \tfrac{1}{16}$$
$$= \tfrac{1}{12} - \tfrac{1}{16} = \tfrac{1}{48}$$

$E[X + Y] = E[X] + E[Y] = \tfrac{4}{3} + \tfrac{1}{4} = \tfrac{19}{12}$

$V[X + Y] = V[X] + V[Y] = \tfrac{2}{9} + \tfrac{1}{48} = \tfrac{35}{144}$

D Some proofs (p. 65)

1D The student's estimate

2 $(1 - q)^{-2} = 1 + (-2)(-q)$
$$+ \dfrac{(-2)(-3)}{2!}(-q)^2 + \dots$$
$$= 1 + 2q + 3q^2 + \dots$$

3E $E[X] = \dfrac{0e^{-\lambda}\lambda^0}{0!} + \dfrac{1e^{-\lambda}\lambda}{1!}$
$$+ \dfrac{2e^{-\lambda}\lambda^2}{2!} + \dfrac{3e^{-\lambda}\lambda^3}{3!} + \dots$$
$$= e^{-\lambda}\left(\lambda + \dfrac{2\lambda^2}{2!} + \dfrac{3\lambda^3}{3!} + \dots\right)$$
$$= \lambda e^{-\lambda}\left(1 + \dfrac{\lambda}{1!} + \dfrac{\lambda^2}{2!} + \dots\right)$$
$$= \lambda e^{-\lambda}e^{\lambda} = \lambda$$

4E Taking the right-hand side of this equation,
$$E[X(X-1)] + E[X] = E[X^2 - X] + E[X]$$
$$= E[X^2] - E[X] + E[X] = E[X^2]$$

5E (a) $E[X(X-1)] = \sum_i i(i-1)P(X = i)$
$$= 2 \times 1e^{-\lambda}\dfrac{\lambda^2}{2!} + 3 \times 2e^{-\lambda}\dfrac{\lambda^3}{3!}$$
$$+ 4 \times 3e^{-\lambda}\dfrac{\lambda^4}{4!} + \dots$$
$$= \lambda^2 e^{-\lambda}\left(1 + \dfrac{\lambda}{1!} + \dfrac{\lambda^2}{2!} + \dots\right)$$
$$= \lambda^2 e^{-\lambda}e^{\lambda} = \lambda^2$$

(b) $V[X] = E[X(X-1)] + E[X] - (E[X])^2$
$$= \lambda^2 + \lambda - \lambda^2 = \lambda$$

6E (a) $E[X] = \int_0^\infty xf(x)\,dx$

$= \lambda \int_0^\infty xe^{-\lambda x}\,dx$

$= [-xe^{-\lambda x}]_0^\infty + \int_0^\infty e^{-\lambda x}\,dx$

(using integration by parts)

$= \left[-\dfrac{1}{\lambda}e^{-\lambda x}\right]_0^\infty$

$= \dfrac{1}{\lambda}$

(b) $V[X] = \int_0^\infty x^2\,f(x)\,dx - (\text{mean})^2$

$= \lambda \int_0^\infty x^2 e^{-\lambda x}\,dx - \left(\dfrac{1}{\lambda}\right)^2$

Again, integration by parts (where you can use your results from (a)) leads to $V[X] = \dfrac{1}{\lambda^2}$

E Combining Normal random variables (p. 67)

Exercise E (p. 70)

1 $X \sim N(14, 0.02),\ Y \sim N(9, 0.01)$

Let the total length be L.

$L = X + Y \sim N(23, 0.03)$

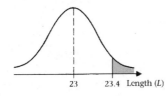

Standardising, $z = \dfrac{23.4 - 23}{\sqrt{0.03}}$

$= 2.31$

$P(L > 23.4) = 1 - \Phi(2.31)$

$= 0.0104$

2 $X \sim N(3, 0.003),\ Y \sim N(20, 0.06)$

Let the total length of the cap plus bottle be L.

$L = X + Y \sim N(23, 0.063)$

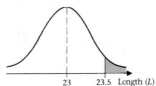

Standardising, $z = \dfrac{23.5 - 23}{\sqrt{0.063}}$

$= 1.99$

$P(L > 23.5) = 1 - \Phi(1.99)$

$= 0.0233$

2.33% will not fit on the shelf.

3 $X \sim N(1.9, 0.01)$

$X + X + \ldots \sim N(12 \times 1.9, 12 \times 0.01)$

$\sim N(22.8, 0.12)$

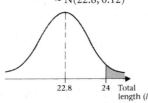

Standardising, $z = \dfrac{24 - 22.8}{\sqrt{0.12}}$

$= 3.46$

$P(L > 24) = 1 - \Phi(3.46)$

$= 0.0003$

0.03% of boxes are too small.

4 $X \sim N(79, 1.25)$

$X + X + \ldots \sim N(5 \times 79, 5 \times 1.25)$

$\sim N(395, 6.25)$

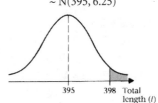

$z = \dfrac{398 - 395}{\sqrt{6.25}}$

$= 1.20$

$P(L \leqslant 398) = \Phi(1.20)$

$= 0.885$

5 $X \sim N(10, 0.013)$, $Y \sim N(9.5, 0.013)$

$X - Y \sim N(0.5, 0.026)$

(a)

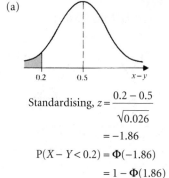

Standardising, $z = \dfrac{0.2 - 0.5}{\sqrt{0.026}}$

$= -1.86$

$P(X - Y < 0.2) = \Phi(-1.86)$

$= 1 - \Phi(1.86)$

$= 0.0314$

3.14% of bolts jam.

(b)

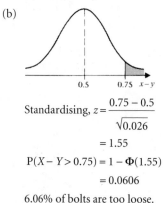

Standardising, $z = \dfrac{0.75 - 0.5}{\sqrt{0.026}}$

$= 1.55$

$P(X - Y > 0.75) = 1 - \Phi(1.55)$

$= 0.0606$

6.06% of bolts are too loose.

6 $X \sim N(18, 0.005)$, $Y \sim N(18.2, 0.005)$

$Y - X \sim N(0.2, 0.01)$

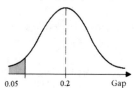

Standardising, $z = \dfrac{0.05 - 0.2}{\sqrt{0.01}}$

$= -1.5$

$P(\text{gap} < 0.05) = \Phi(-1.5)$

$= 1 - \Phi(1.5)$

$= 0.0668$

6.68% of lids do not fit.

6 Hypothesis testing

A Making a decision: the null hypothesis (p. 72)

1D (a) If the dice is 'fair', the number of sixes out of 60 is $R \sim B(60, \frac{1}{6})$.

The Normal approximation is $X \sim N(10, 8\frac{1}{3})$.

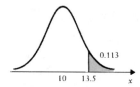

$P(R \geqslant 14) \approx P(X > 13.5)$

$\approx P\left(Z > \dfrac{13.5 - 10}{\sqrt{8\frac{1}{3}}} \right)$

$\approx P(Z > 1.212) \approx 0.113$

There is a probability of 0.113 that a fair dice will be wrongly classified as 'loaded'.

(b) If the dice is 'loaded', the number of sixes out of 60 is $R \sim B(60, \frac{1}{4})$.

The Normal approximation is $X \sim N(15, 11\frac{1}{4})$.

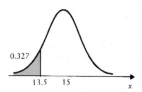

$P(R < 14) \approx P(X < 13.5)$

$\approx P\left(Z < \dfrac{13.5 - 15}{\sqrt{11\frac{1}{4}}} \right)$

$\approx P(Z < -0.447) \approx 0.327$

There is a probability of 0.327 that a biased dice will be wrongly accepted as 'fair'.

(c) (i) If the threshold is changed to 13, for a fair dice, $X \sim N(10, 8\frac{1}{3})$.

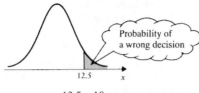

Probability of a wrong decision

$$z = \frac{12.5 - 10}{\sqrt{8\frac{1}{3}}} = 0.866$$

$P(Z > 0.866) = 0.193$

The probability of wrongly classifying a fair dice as 'loaded' is

$P(Z > 0.866) \approx 0.193$

The probability of wrongly classifying a loaded dice as 'fair' is

$P(Z < -0.745) \approx 0.229$

(ii) The probability of wrongly classifying the dice as 'loaded' $\approx P(Z > 1.559) \approx 0.059$

The probability of wrongly classifying the dice as 'fair' $\approx P(Z < -0.149) \approx 0.440$

(iii) The 'best' threshold value is open to discussion.

(d) Although it would be very unlikely that a number as low as (or lower than) this might occur, it is possible. It is unlikely to happen if the dice is 'fair', but it is even more unlikely to happen with a 'loaded' dice, so you should conclude that the dice is 'fair'.

2D The student's friend only claims to be able to 'taste the difference'. If she had none correct, she would have identified every one incorrectly. She could still claim to be able to 'taste the difference'; she simply did not know which was which. The correct alternative hypothesis in this case is $H_1 : p \neq \frac{1}{2}$.

B   Making the wrong decision (p. 73)

1 $P(X > 10) = P\left(Z > \dfrac{10 - 6.2}{1.8}\right)$

$= P(Z > 2.111)$

≈ 0.0174

2 The probability of a type II error is

$$P\left(Z < \frac{10 - \mu}{\sigma}\right).$$

You cannot evaluate this unless you know μ and σ.

3 $P(X > 9) \approx P(Z > 1556) \approx 0.060$

4 The probability of a type II error will decrease.

5 $P(Z > 1.645) = 0.05$ so

$$\frac{x - 6.2}{1.8} = 1.645 \Rightarrow x = 9.161$$

C   Level of significance (p. 74)

(a)

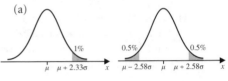

(b)

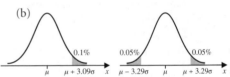

Exercise C (p. 78)

1 $H_0 : p = \frac{1}{5}$
$H_1 : p > \frac{1}{5}$
Level of significance: 5%

If $R \sim B(120, \frac{1}{5})$ then the Normal approximation is $X \sim N(24, 19.2)$. The critical region is $X > 24 + 1.645\sqrt{19.2}$ or $X > 31.2$.

H_0 is rejected if $R \geq 32$. A candidate is unlikely to be answering purely by guesswork if he or she obtains 32 or more correct answers.

2 The null hypothesis is that the probability that a digit is even is $\frac{1}{2}$.

$H_0 : p = \frac{1}{2}$
$H_1 : p \neq \frac{1}{2}$

Level of significance: 5%

If R is the number of even digits out of fourteen, then $R \sim B(14, \frac{1}{2})$.

The data give $R = 4$. This is obviously not in the upper critical region but could be in the lower critical region.

$P(R \leqslant 4) \approx 0.09$. This is greater than $2\frac{1}{2}\%$ and so H_0 is *not* rejected.

3    $H_0 : \mu = 1300$
     $H_1 : \mu < 1300$

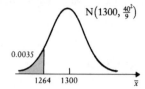

$N\left(1300, \frac{40^2}{9}\right)$

0.0035

1264   1300 $\bar{x}$

The data give $\bar{x} = 1264$

$P(\bar{X} < 1264) = P(Z < -2.7)$
≈ 0.0035

This is significant at the 1% level but not the 0.1% level. There is very significant evidence that the breaking strain is lower than expected.

4   If the machine is out of adjustment then the mean can be either too large or too small, so a two-tail test is appropriate.

$H_0 : \mu = 3.00$
$H_1 : \mu \neq 3.00$

Level of significance: 5%

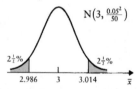

$N\left(3, \frac{0.05^2}{50}\right)$

$2\frac{1}{2}\%$ $2\frac{1}{2}\%$

2.986   3   3.014 $\bar{x}$

As $3.01 < 3.014$, $\bar{x} = 3.01$ is *not* in the critical region; therefore H_0 is not rejected at the 5% level of significance. The machine does not need adjusting.

5    $H_0 : \mu = 0.85$
     $H_1 : \mu > 0.85$

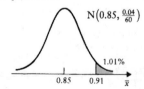

$N\left(0.85, \frac{0.04}{60}\right)$

1.01%

0.85   0.91 $\bar{x}$

$P(\bar{X} > 0.91) = P\left(Z > \dfrac{0.91 - 0.85}{\sqrt{\frac{0.04}{60}}}\right)$

$= P(Z > 2.324)$
≈ 0.0101

The result is in the 'significant' 5% critical region but not quite in the 'very significant' 1% critical region. The evidence would therefore be described as 'significant'. (You should note that the sample mean, $\bar{x} = 0.91$, has probably been rounded. A more accurate value could be used and the evidence might then become 'very significant'.)

6   The most appropriate model for S, the number of patients per thousand requiring surgery, is a Poisson distribution.

$S \sim P(\lambda)$

$H_0 : \lambda = 14$
$H_1 : \lambda < 14$

Level of significance: 1%

$P(S \leqslant 6) = e^{-14} + 14e^{-14} + \dfrac{14^2 e^{-14}}{2!}$

$\qquad = + \ldots + \dfrac{14^6 e^{-14}}{6!}$

$\qquad = 0.0142$

H_0 is accepted at the 1% level of significance, and the next level of testing should not go ahead without further evidence of benefit to patients.

$P(S \leqslant 5) = 0.0055$. This result is significant at the 1% level.

7   The number of items lost per week can be modelled using the Poisson distribution, $L \sim P(100)$, but because $\lambda = 100$ is large, this can be approximated using the Normal distribution, which will make the calculation of probabilities easier.

$L \sim N(100, 100)$

A 5% level of significance is selected.

$H_0 : \lambda = 100$
$H_1 : \lambda < 100$

Level of significance: 5%

Using the Normal distribution

$P(L < 70.5) = P\left(Z < \dfrac{82.5 - 100}{10}\right)$

$\qquad = P(Z < -1.75)$
$\qquad = 0.04$

The reported level of losses is significant at the 5% level, and indicates that the new supervisor has improved baggage handling at the airport.

Tables

Students should familiarise themselves with the tables which will be provided for the examination. Layouts, numbers of significant figures and definitions of probabilities can all vary.

Table 1 The Standard Normal distribution

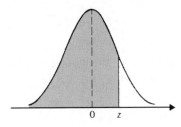

The table on the next page gives the area to the left of (or below) any given z-value. z is the number of standard deviations from the mean value.

z	0.00	0.01	0.02	0.03	0.04	0.05	0.06	0.07	0.08	0.09
0.0	0.5000	0.5040	0.5080	0.5120	0.5160	0.5199	0.5239	0.5279	0.5319	0.5359
0.1	0.5398	0.5438	0.5478	0.5517	0.5557	0.5596	0.5636	0.5675	0.5714	0.5753
0.2	0.5793	0.5832	0.5871	0.5910	0.5948	0.5987	0.6026	0.6064	0.6103	0.6141
0.3	0.6179	0.6217	0.6255	0.6293	0.6331	0.6368	0.6406	0.6443	0.6480	0.6517
0.4	0.6554	0.6591	0.6628	0.6664	0.6700	0.6736	0.6772	0.6808	0.6844	0.6879
0.5	0.6915	0.6950	0.6985	0.7019	0.7054	0.7088	0.7123	0.7157	0.7190	0.7224
0.6	0.7257	0.7291	0.7324	0.7357	0.7389	0.7422	0.7454	0.7486	0.7517	0.7549
0.7	0.7580	0.7611	0.7642	0.7673	0.7704	0.7734	0.7764	0.7794	0.7823	0.7852
0.8	0.7881	0.7910	0.7939	0.7967	0.7995	0.8023	0.8051	0.8078	0.8106	0.8133
0.9	0.8159	0.8186	0.8212	0.8238	0.8264	0.8289	0.8315	0.8340	0.8365	0.8389
1.0	0.8413	0.8438	0.8461	0.8485	0.8508	0.8531	0.8554	0.8577	0.8599	0.8621
1.1	0.8643	0.8665	0.8686	0.8708	0.8729	0.8749	0.8770	0.8790	0.8810	0.8830
1.2	0.8849	0.8869	0.8888	0.8907	0.8925	0.8944	0.8962	0.8980	0.8997	0.9015
1.3	0.9032	0.9049	0.9066	0.9082	0.9099	0.9115	0.9131	0.9147	0.9162	0.9177
1.4	0.9192	0.9207	0.9222	0.9236	0.9251	0.9265	0.9279	0.9292	0.9306	0.9319
1.5	0.9332	0.9345	0.9357	0.9370	0.9382	0.9394	0.9406	0.9418	0.9429	0.9441
1.6	0.9452	0.9463	0.9474	0.9484	0.9495	0.9505	0.9515	0.9525	0.9535	0.9545
1.7	0.9554	0.9564	0.9573	0.9582	0.9591	0.9599	0.9608	0.9616	0.9625	0.9633
1.8	0.9641	0.9649	0.9656	0.9664	0.9671	0.9678	0.9686	0.9693	0.9699	0.9706
1.9	0.9713	0.9719	0.9726	0.9732	0.9738	0.9744	0.9750	0.9756	0.9761	0.9767
2.0	0.9772	0.9778	0.9783	0.9788	0.9793	0.9798	0.9803	0.9808	0.9812	0.9817
2.1	0.9821	0.9826	0.9830	0.9834	0.9838	0.9842	0.9846	0.9850	0.9854	0.9857
2.2	0.9861	0.9864	0.9868	0.9871	0.9875	0.9878	0.9881	0.9884	0.9887	0.9890
2.3	0.9893	0.9896	0.9898	0.9901	0.9904	0.9906	0.9909	0.9911	0.9913	0.9916
2.4	0.9918	0.9920	0.9922	0.9925	0.9927	0.9929	0.9931	0.9932	0.9934	0.9936
2.5	0.9938	0.9940	0.9941	0.9943	0.9945	0.9946	0.9948	0.9949	0.9951	0.9952
2.6	0.9953	0.9955	0.9956	0.9957	0.9959	0.9960	0.9961	0.9962	0.9963	0.9964
2.7	0.9965	0.9966	0.9967	0.9968	0.9969	0.9970	0.9971	0.9972	0.9973	0.9974
2.8	0.9974	0.9975	0.9976	0.9977	0.9977	0.9978	0.9979	0.9979	0.9980	0.9981
2.9	0.9981	0.9982	0.9982	0.9983	0.9984	0.9984	0.9985	0.9985	0.9986	0.9986
3.0	0.9987	0.9987	0.9987	0.9988	0.9988	0.9989	0.9989	0.9989	0.9990	0.9990
3.1	0.9990	0.9991	0.9991	0.9991	0.9992	0.9992	0.9992	0.9992	0.9993	0.9993
3.2	0.9993	0.9993	0.9994	0.9994	0.9994	0.9994	0.9994	0.9995	0.9995	0.9995
3.3	0.9995	0.9995	0.9995	0.9996	0.9996	0.9996	0.9996	0.9996	0.9996	0.9997
3.4	0.9997	0.9997	0.9997	0.9997	0.9997	0.9997	0.9997	0.9997	0.9997	0.9998

Table 2 Upper percentage points for chi-squared distributions

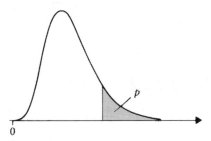

The tabulated value is χ_p^2, where $P(X^2 > \chi_p^2) = p$, when X^2 has a χ^2 distribution with v degrees of freedom.

The tables provided for use in the examination may also give lower percentage points, and may define p as $P(X^2 < \chi_p^2) = p$.

p		0.1	0.05	0.025	0.01	0.005	0.001
$v =$	1	2.71	3.84	5.02	6.63	7.88	10.83
	2	4.61	5.99	7.38	9.21	10.60	13.81
	3	6.25	7.81	9.35	11.34	12.84	16.27
	4	7.78	9.49	11.14	13.28	14.86	18.47
	5	9.24	11.07	12.83	15.09	16.75	20.52
	6	10.64	12.59	14.45	16.81	18.55	22.46
	7	12.02	14.07	16.01	18.48	20.28	24.32
	8	13.36	15.51	17.53	20.09	21.95	26.12
	9	14.68	16.92	19.02	21.67	23.59	27.88
	10	15.99	18.31	20.48	23.21	25.19	29.59
	12	18.55	21.03	23.34	26.22	28.30	32.91
	14	21.06	23.68	26.12	29.14	31.32	36.12
	16	23.54	26.30	28.85	32.00	34.27	39.25
	18	25.99	28.87	31.53	34.81	37.16	42.31
	20	28.41	31.41	34.17	37.57	40.00	45.31
	25	34.38	37.65	40.65	44.31	46.93	52.62
	30	40.26	43.77	46.98	50.89	53.67	59.70
	40	51.81	55.76	59.34	63.69	66.77	73.40
	50	63.17	67.50	71.42	76.15	79.49	86.66
	60	74.40	79.08	83.30	88.38	91.95	99.61
	100	118.5	124.3	129.6	135.8	140.2	149.4

Index